Microsoft Content Management Server Field Guide

■ ■ ■

François-Paul Briand and
Michael Wirsching

Apress®

Microsoft Content Management Server Field Guide

Copyright © 2005 by François-Paul Briand and Michael Wirsching

Lead Editor: Jim Sumser
Technical Reviewers: Dan P. Dougherty and Judith Myerson
Editorial Board: Steve Anglin, Dan Appleman, Ewan Buckingham, Gary Cornell, Tony Davis,
    Jason Gilmore, Jonathan Hassell, Chris Mills, Dominic Shakeshaft, Jim Sumser
Associate Publisher: Grace Wong
Project Manager: Laura Cheu
Copy Edit Manager: Nicole LeClerc
Copy Editor: Julie McNamee
Production Manager: Kari Brooks-Copony
Production Editor: Linda Marousek
Compositor: Linda Weidemann
Proofreader: Liz Welch
Indexer: John Collin
Artist: Kinetic Publishing Services, LLC
Cover Designer: Kurt Krames
Manufacturing Manager: Tom Debolski

Library of Congress Cataloging-in-Publication Data

Briand, François-Paul, 1954–
    Microsoft Content Management Server field guide / François-Paul Briand and Michael
Wirsching.
        p.   cm.
    Includes index.
    ISBN 1-59059-528-9
    1. Microsoft Content management server (Electronic resource) 2. Web sites—Design—
Computer programs. 3. Web sites—Management—Computer programs. 4. Database
management. I. Wirsching, Michael. II. Title.
TK5105.8885.M52B75   2005
005.2'76—dc22

                                                                        2005014408

ISBN (pbk): 1-59059-528-9

Printed and bound in the United States of America 9 8 7 6 5 4 3 2 1

Trademarked names may appear in this book. Rather than use a trademark symbol with
every occurrence of a trademarked name, we use the names only in an editorial fashion and
to the benefit of the trademark owner, with no intention of infringement of the trademark.

Distributed to the book trade in the United States by Springer-Verlag New York, Inc., 233
Spring Street, 6th Floor, New York, NY 10013, and outside the United States by Springer-
Verlag GmbH & Co. KG, Tiergartenstr. 17, 69112 Heidelberg, Germany.

In the United States: phone 1-800-SPRINGER, fax 201-348-4505, e-mail orders@springer-
ny.com, or visit http://www.springer-ny.com. Outside the United States: fax +49 6221
345229, e-mail orders@springer.de, or visit http://www.springer.de.

For information on translations, please contact Apress directly at 2560 Ninth Street, Suite
219, Berkeley, CA 94710. Phone 510-549-5930, fax 510-549-5939, e-mail info@apress.com,
or visit http://www.apress.com.

The information in this book is distributed on an "as is" basis, without warranty. Although every
precaution has been taken in the preparation of this work, neither the author(s) nor Apress
shall have any liability to any person or entity with respect to any loss or damage caused or
alleged to be caused directly or indirectly by the information contained in this work.

A mon père, François Luc Briand,
qui a toujours instillé en moi l'amour
du travail bien fait.

—François-Paul Briand

Contents at a Glance

PART 1 ▪▪▪ Configuration

PART 2 ▪▪▪ Administration and Deployment

PART 3 ▪▪▪ Templates

Contents

PART 1 ▪▪▪ Configuration

PART 2 ■■■ Administration and Deployment

PART 3 ■ ■ ■ Templates

About the Authors

François-Paul Briand and **Mike Wirsching** develop business solutions called Learning Instruments, which embed training into the user interface.

 Co-founder and president of BWI, **François-Paul Briand** is a computer architect who was, in no small part, responsible for moving forensic biometrics from mid-sized systems to distributed personal computing environments with open standards (HTTP, XML). Under François-Paul's guidance, BWI has developed commercial software products for the training and biometric security markets. BWI also provides consulting services on a contract basis and custom products in various segments of the software industry.

 Trained in engineering and behavioral science, **Mike Wirsching**'s passion is considering how thinking can be mediated by computers. Embedding training into the UI has been his forte since he was an instructional designer at Microsoft.

BWI's inspiration for a UI that teaches thinking is drawn from psychologists and educators such as Reuven Feuerstein (Instrumental Enrichment), Howard Gardiner (Multiple Intelligences), Barbara Clark (Optimizing Learning), and Edward de Bono (PMI Thinking Technique).

About the Technical Reviewers

 **Daniel P. Dougherty**, P.E., is a registered professional engineer. Dan earned bachelor degrees in Electrical Engineering and Business Administration from the University of Washington in 1976. Since then, Dan has been involved in the soup-to-nuts design and implementation of industrial control and information systems for manufacturers of a wide range of products, including foods, beverages, and airplanes.

In recent years, he has focused on the collection and analysis of factory-floor data to help increase manufacturing productivity. Each industrial control and information systems project requires a classic, make-versus-buy decision to meet customer requirements. Typically, Dan has configured commercially available, off-the-shelf industrial software solutions to meet most of the requirements, and developed remaining requirements with standard Microsoft programming and database tools.

Dan is a current member and retired board member of the .NET Developers Association, a .NET User Group in the Seattle area.

Judith Myerson is a systems architect and engineer. Areas of interest include middleware technologies, enterprise-wide systems, database technologies, application development, server/network management, security, firewall technologies, information assurance, operating systems, and project management. She reviewed *Hardening Linux* published by Apress in early 2005.

Introduction

Don't read this!

Don't read this first, anyway. Start anywhere in the book and just read what you need! Read this only if you want to know why we did or didn't do something later in the text.

What is this book about? This book is about the tasks required to configure and operate a Web site based on Microsoft Content Management Server 2002. When we say this book is about creating a Web site, we're talking about a content-rich site that supports a specific business need—and the attendant community of workers—with a cogent interface. According to Microsoft, such a site is termed a *portal*. Microsoft Content Management Server (MCMS) is part of Microsoft's integrated portal technologies, that is, products providing a comprehensive Web Services framework.

What is Content Management Server? MCMS enables companies to rapidly develop, deploy, and maintain content-rich, highly volatile Web sites. An MCMS site is actually a site within a site—one site faces the world and its shadow image provides access to users whose job is to contribute content to the site. MCMS provides tools to implement and administer both the production and development environments.

The MCMS content-management strategy hinges upon empowering a community of workers to author content, schedule updates, and administer a site, on its own—all while maintaining consistent quality and accessibility. MCMS provides tools for organizing and automating dynamic content delivery. In fact, MCMS allows an organization to define specific roles (author, editor, approver, administrator, and so on), assign them to various users, and automate each user's experience with data views and tools based on the user's job role. You might say that all this can be done with scripted Web pages, so where's the big value? Efficiency. MCMS abstracts Web content from markup language (HTML) by providing a behind-the-scenes page-rendering framework. With this approach, the same content is easily repurposed, filtered, and personalized programmatically, using tools and components provided by MCMS. IT creates the rules and field personnel manage the site's content.

What problems are being solved? Some Web sites are hungrier for content than others—think about a site supporting a news agency, trade periodical, or a technical-readiness e-learning site. Updates to the site must be posted continually: new information must be added and out-of-date content must be removed (or archived). It's a massive IT chore. First content has to be developed and acquired. Next it must be formatted for display on Web pages. Along the way, navigation has to be adjusted to accommodate the changing site landscape. The guys and gals in the IT trenches will tell you how much data are dumped into their laps everyday. Rather than forcing data through this IT bottleneck, however, wouldn't it be better to distribute the content posting effort? What if each worker on the front line gathered and submitted content directly? What if editorial and administrative resources close to the business problem—not the server technology—scheduled updates and managed business content? Solving problems such as this is raison d'etre for the Content Management Server.

Among the many case studies that Microsoft has published, a study of a mid-sized health care company that creates medical training and marketing collateral is a good example of a CMS win. Producing the training materials requires intensive collaboration from groups of biotech workers residing in partner firms located around the world. The Microsoft Office–based, MCMS portal solution sped up production and editorial processes and minimized the previous—and very costly—paper-based practices. The result was increased revenue for the health care company because it was able to take on additional projects.

Let's conclude the discussion of what problems are solved by taking a step back. Even though MCMS is a server technology that is employed in a transparent (to users) way, it's still a "user" technology. The goal may be lessening the load on an overworked IT department, but the means is to personalize each user's experience.

The Big Picture: Portals

A portal is a Web site that aggregates contextually relevant information and services. In short, a portal distills knowledge from data. The right portal transforms how and how effectively a corporation conducts its business. Why portals? Portals allow multiple layers of security. Content resources are abstracted from page markup. User roles restrict general access. Portals provide a mechanism that supports personalization. Personalization is blended from a mix of UI preferences and programmatic rules. Portals facilitate application integration by interconnecting systems through data sharing and automated transactions. Portals allow information workers to create content once, reuse that content, and gather content from disparate sources to display within a single interface.

A CMS portal automates content approval and publication. CMS enables knowledge workers to combine efforts—synchronously and asynchronously through meeting spaces, project sites, automated workflow, document check-in/checkout, IM, polls, subscriptions, and alerts.

According to Microsoft, portals are increasingly more common. Creating and maintaining a portal, however, represents a substantial technical challenge, which is why Microsoft released its integrated portal technologies (MIPT). MIPT is a group of common architectural elements that provide a comprehensive framework to meet business needs. Microsoft products and platforms address portal requirements through a layered architecture, provided by Microsoft Server 2003 and SQL Server. On top of the platform layer comes the Web application platform: developer tools and a rendering/application-integration framework. The Web application and base layers combined provide a platform on which any Web service can be built.

CMS: A Rendering Framework

Microsoft servers enable developers to work with abstracted notions of Web pages (no HTML). The rendering framework is responsible for assembling and rendering pages dynamically.

CMS-VS Common Development Environment

Portals typically require integrating several technologies and developing custom functionality. Significant benefit derives from an integrated stack of technologies coupled with a single development environment. If that development environment is also easy to use and leverages common skills, portal development is faster and cheaper.

How do you implement the solution? We are writing this book from the standpoint of a small- to medium-sized business supporting a content-intensive site. With MCMS, the size of the company is less the issue than the volume of content. MCMS is the proverbial sledgehammer that shouldn't be used to kill fleas. An MCMS solution can be expensive to implement and operate. If the business problem falls in the MCMS sweet spot, implementing MCMS will get you promoted! If MCMS is not a good fit for your business, move along because there's nothing but trouble in this book. So, how do you implement an MCMS solution? An MCMS solution springs from a central server where development is managed. The development server will probably support multiple production servers. In the development environment, the site is designed and the templates are created along with any programmatic customization that is required. The primary configuration and management applications are run from here. With MCMS, the primary customization environment is typically Visual Studio; however, other tools may be substituted. Multiple servers may be required for the development environment and certainly multiple developer client machines. Generally speaking, however, server loads are low and there are few concurrent users.

The production environment, on the other hand, can experience significant loading. We have included a short section on capacity planning, but it is really outside the scope of this book. Just understand that for many enterprise installations where MCMS shines its brightest, the production environment is a server farm, with multiple firewalls, load balancing, failover clustering, and all those other exotic—and expensive—technologies to serve thousands of users and hundreds of concurrent transactions.

Even if your solution doesn't approach that kind of scale, there are plenty of wrinkles you'll need to deal with. Remember an MCMS site is actually a site within a site. There is the site where pages are assembled for denizens of Internet-land to view and there is the site where contributors post content. Further, an MCMS site is dynamic in nature. Page templates contain place-holders for content elements that are extracted either from a database or cache and merged with the templates, and then the entire object is then rendered to the viewer as markup—HTML. In some instances, many relating to non-Microsoft servers, a dynamic site is not an option. MCMS provides a solution to this by allowing the dynamic site to be staged as a static site containing HTML-based pages only (no placeholders to resolve). Read-only sites can be implemented as dynamic or static. Read/write can only be implemented as dynamic; content has to flow bidirectionally—to and from the Content Repository database. Replication must be managed for all the sites in any environment consisting of multiple servers.

Before you undertake the creation of a Web site, we strongly recommend that you write a specification, even if it's just on paper. This, however, is not part of the scope of this book. Neither is running the setup program for the MCMS.

We hope this book serves you as a handy job aid. Unlike most large computer books that contain a lot of information of questionable value to a working professional, this book is small and the writing is sparse in an effort to just provide the operational details that you need to get things done. We hope this book is all you need and not much else.

PART 1

■ ■ ■

Configuration

CHAPTER 1

■ ■ ■

Configuring the Platform

This chapter covers

- Understanding scalable architecture
  - Logical architecture
  - Physical site architecture
- Configuring the Microsoft Content Management Server (MCMS) platform options
  - Checking minimum hardware and software requirements
  - Installing Windows 2003 Server core components
  - Installing Windows XP components
  - Installing SQL Server 2000
  - Enabling Windows Installer logging
- Creating user accounts
  - Initial MCMS administrator
  - Initial MCMS account
- Creating the MCMS database and granting rights
- Creating a Web site for MCMS

This chapter describes the various site architectures that support Microsoft Content Management Server 2002, and why you might choose to configure them. MCMS installation is covered in Chapter 2. Chapter 3 covers techniques for performance tuning and capacity planning. Clustering and high-availability MCMS solutions are not covered in this book.

Understanding Scalable Architecture

Some have difficulty seeing the value of MCMS—what it does differently from a Web server. MCMS turns a Web site into an online document exchange where content is not only presented, but developed as well. In the introduction, we discussed some scenarios where this document exchange is vital to a business. The CMS document exchange paradigm is equally valid for small business or global enterprise. As noted business analyst Peter Drucker points out, a high percentage of the American workforce is made up of knowledge workers. A small business may not have the resources of a mega enterprise; yet its business may depend upon empowering knowledge workers to collaborate on content. MCMS, therefore, supports site architectures geared for each end of this spectrum and many points in between.

MCMS supports single-server installations. In this configuration, the entire content management functionality is implemented on one computer. For many situations this provides adequate throughput and security. At the opposite end of the spectrum, MCMS provides features to support multitiered, clustered, server farms with redundant firewalls, domain security, and shared databases.

MCMS also supports scenarios in which teams of developers work simultaneously on the same—or independent—MCMS projects. Here development machines can be running Windows Server or Windows XP. They can run SQL Server locally or connect to another machine running SQL Server remotely.

This chapter examines the platform requirements to support the various components of MCMS installations. We'll also cover the various configuration options identified in the preceding paragraphs.

Logical Architecture

We'll begin looking at the logical architecture of the MCMS system. Each component is described later in this section; however, let's start with a broad picture.

First, a computer that will be configured to run MCMS must also be running a version of Windows: Windows Server 2003 (in this chapter, we'll be referring to Windows 2003 unless otherwise stated), Windows Server 2000 (only covered peripherally), or Windows XP. Specific details about configuring the Windows operating system are outside the scope of this book, except where noted. Note that SQL Server must either be present locally or available remotely.

To the left side of Figure 1-1, you'll note *development* components: Visual Studio, custom Web Services, and the ASPX templates. Visual Studio has tools for managing the development of MCMS solutions, including creating the templates. (Creating templates is covered in Chapter 9.)

Components for accessing content are shown in the top center of the figure. These components are used by authors and viewers—viewers, in the MCMS vernacular are called *subscribers*. This is managed via the HTTP transaction processor of the Internet Information Server (IIS) Web Service and a custom MCMS ISAPI filter (covered in Chapter 9).

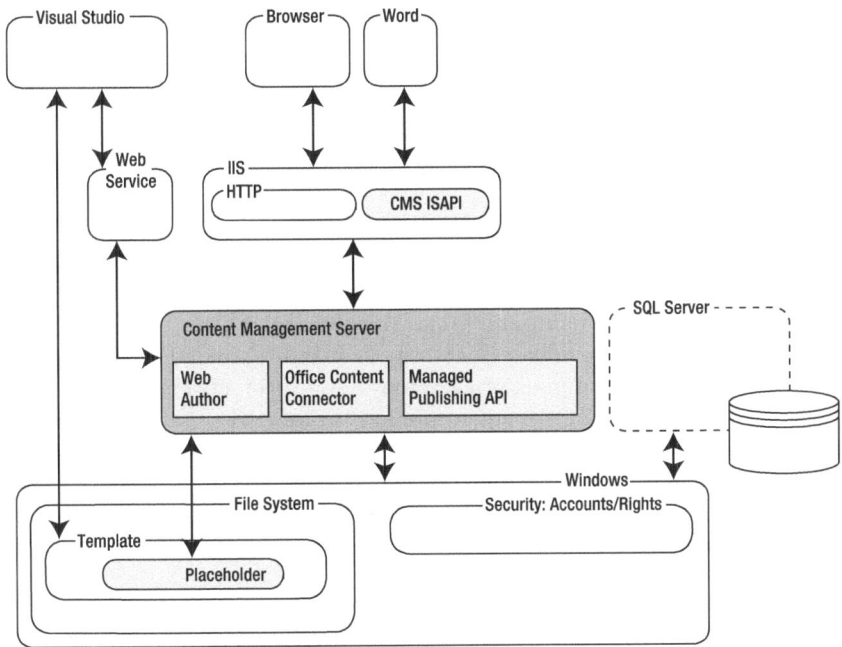

Figure 1-1. *MCMS components*

The components of the logical architecture are defined in the following list:

- **ASPX template file:** Placeholders, controls, and so on.

- **Authoring Connector:** Enables authors to create content and send content directly to MCMS for publication using Microsoft Office.

- **Content Repository:** Microsoft SQL Server database (table definitions, stored procedures); stores information about site structure and content, including resources.

- **Content server:** The core MCMS engine.

- **Custom Web Service:** An MCMS extension to allow a Web application to interact with MCMS.

- **ISAPI filter and security service**: Serves HTTP requests for the MCMS Web site, handles authentication of these requests, creates the context in which ASPX template files run, and assembles the page.

- **Placeholder control**: Provides data access to the Content Repository and resources.

- **Publishing API**: Provides programmatic access to the MCMS object model used by placeholder control(s) to access and negotiate authoring mode.

- **Visual Studio .NET**: Main development environment supports the various extensions that exploit MCMS features and objects.

- **Web author**: The main authoring application for MCMS 2002.

Physical Site Architecture

Figure 1-2 shows a typical MCMS site installation. A high-volume production environment is implemented across an indeterminately large bank of servers—from a single server handling everything to an entire clustered server farm. The production environment may or may not be protected behind an external firewall. The production environment is supported by a development/content-authoring environment, which should be protected behind its own firewall. This environment is built up from a single development server, which is configured first and can replicate the implementation to the other systems.

Following are the servers shown in Figure 1-2:

- **Development server**: Contains content database and templates; used in content rendering; relatively few authorized users access this server.

- **Content authoring server**: Used by contributors to submit content; authors, editors, approvers, and administrators access this server to manage content development.

- **Staging server**: Provides a platform where content is tested before it is deployed to the production environment; access to this server is similar to the content authoring server.

- **Production server(s)**: Provides the live site where users access content.

Note A third deployment option, which is outside the scope of this book, is using the Site Deployment API in conjunction with Microsoft Application Center 2000 to perform incremental deployments. This is for non-MCMS sites (ASP.NET-based sites). Refer to COM-Based Site Deployment in the MCMS product documentation for more information.

For additional information about Application Center 2000, go to http://go.
microsoft.com/fwlink/?LinkId=9514.

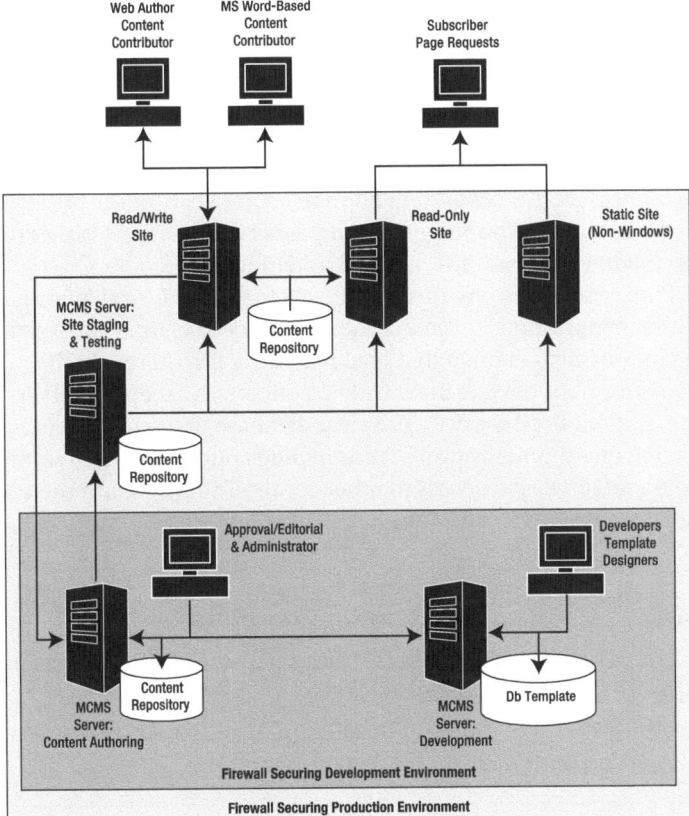

Figure 1-2. *A typical MCMS installation*

Figure 1-2 also implies how workflow progresses. MCMS is deployed to the *development server*, providing initial administration and the ability to create the site structure, including the content database and templates. The site is replicated to the *authoring server* so contributors can post their content (depending upon the total expected volume, the authoring and development servers may coexist on a single computer). Many authors generally update this MCMS frequently. Security and authentication can be time consuming in the initial stages because individuals and groups of collaborators may be restricted to certain parts of the site.

The next step—and again, this can all be configured on a single computer—is to implement the staging server that will support the production environment. Initially, and periodically thereafter, an administrator replicates content from the authoring server to the staging server—usually at scheduled intervals. At this point, the production site can be tested and prepared for general access. Typically production servers provide dynamic access to content; however, some servers may need to serve static HTML pages. The site staging server, therefore, may need to convert dynamic content to static HTML for some servers.

Finally the production environment is implemented. The complexity of this chore can vary vastly, depending upon the complexity of the business solution. If a production environment encompasses relatively few (single) servers and is tolerant of downtime, manual updating is adequate. On the other hand, if the production environment needs to be highly available and not at all tolerant of downtime, this may require failover clustering and redundancy. Traffic may be high enough that load balancing is required. In the production environment, servers may work in concert, with certain servers deploying the Content Repository (SQL Server database) for general access. Some production environments provide anonymous public access to some shared content and privileged access to other content. Some environments require a high degree of personalization.

■Note Follow the installation steps in this section to install platform software if you do not have a previous version of MCMS on your computer. If you have MCMS 2001 installed on your computer, you must follow a different set of steps to upgrade to MCMS 2002. For information about upgrading to MCMS 2002 from MCMS 2001, see the upgrading instructions at http://go.microsoft.com/fwlink/?LinkId=9919.

The steps to install the platform software must be completed in the order presented in this chapter. Before you install MCMS 2002, check to see if you have already installed the required software.

To install MCMS 2002, you must be a member of the Windows NT administrators group.

Configuring MCMS Platform Options

This chapter is a quick reference and does not cover all details of the installation. It does not cover versions of Windows Server other than 2003, though MCMS 2002 can be configured to interoperate with some other versions. We'll also cover configuring Windows XP to support MCMS 2002, which is useful for development machines.

MCMS 2002 SP1a is compatible with and can be installed on Windows Server 2003 and Windows XP.

■**Note** MCMS 2002 SP1a is not supported on Windows Server 2003 Web Edition or Windows Server 2003 Datacenter Edition.

For the purpose of this book, assume that we're referring to MCMS 2002 SP1a installed on Windows 2003 Server, unless otherwise noted. The configuration instructions provided in this chapter refer to the following editions of MCMS 2002 with SP1a:

- **Evaluation Edition**: Includes features of Enterprise Edition; stops processing after 120 days.

- **Developer Edition**: Includes features of Enterprise Edition; for development teams that build sites only and is not licensed for production environments.

- **Standard Edition**: Small- or medium-sized organizations/departments; only supports a single processor, limited server clustering, 15 authorized users, and no support for staging.

■**Note** Staging is the automated conversion of MCMS dynamic ASPs (Active Server Pages) to static HTML.

- **Enterprise Edition**: Large installations; supports multiple processors, clustering, unlimited number of rights groups and users, and staging.

We also assume that you have MCMS 2002 SP1a; however, if you are evaluating the product, you may find it useful to refer to the MCMS 2002 with SP1a Help, which is available at `http://go.microsoft.com/fwlink/?LinkId=9919`.

Check Minimum Hardware and Software Requirements

Following are the hardware requirements to install and run MCMS 2002 on a single computer:

- PC with Pentium III-compatible or higher processor
- 1GB of RAM
- 2GB of free disk space (MCMS only)
- CD-ROM drive
- Network Interface Card (NIC)

Installing Windows 2003 Server Core Components

> **Note** MCMS 2002 with SP1a is not supported on Windows Server 2003 Web Edition or Windows Server 2003 Datacenter Edition. If the IIS 6.0 components were installed with IIS Web Server Extensions, you must use Add/Remove Programs to remove them and add them again.

You need to install IIS 6.0 components (which are included but not installed by default) before you install MCMS 2002 or MCMS 2002 with SP1a:

- IIS 6.0
- ASP.NET
- ASP
- Server Side includes

Task 1-1. Installing Server Side Includes

1. Select Add/Remove Windows Components (Add/Remove Programs), select Application Server, and then select Details.
2. Select Internet Information Services in the Application Server dialog box, and then select Details.
3. Select World Wide Web Service in the Internet Information Services dialog box, and then select Details.
4. Select the Server Side Includes from the World Wide Web Service dialog box.
5. Finish the Windows Components Wizard dialog box.

> **Note** The .NET Framework 1.1 is installed with Windows Server 2003. .NET Framework 1.0 does not adversely affect the Windows Server 2003 system; however, MCMS 2002 with SP1a only works with .NET Framework 1.1.

Task 1-2. Enabling IIS

1. Select Add/Remove Windows Components (Add/Remove Programs on the Control Panel).

2. Select Internet Information Services (IIS) and Details. Check the boxes to add the following components:

   • Common Files

   • Internet Information Services Snap-In

   • World Wide Web Server

Installing Windows XP Components

Install Windows XP and the latest service pack. You also need to install Visual Studio 2003 to provide the .NET Framework 1.1 and other development tools as follows:

• IIS 5.0

• ASP.NET

• ASP

Note IIS 5.0 is installed with Windows XP. Although it is compatible, you need to configure MCMS under the default Web site. The version of IIS installed and supported by Windows XP will not allow you to create multiple Web sites.

Installing SQL Server 2000

Note If you are evaluating MCMS, you can also install SQL Server 2000 evaluation software.

Microsoft recommends configuring SQL Server 2000 with the latest service pack (SP3a).

Note SP3a can be downloaded from http://go.microsoft.com/fwlink/ ?LinkId=13955). MCMS 2002 SP1a isn't supported on SQL Server 7.0.

If you don't have SQL Server operating, select Create a New Instance of SQL Server, and install the following components:

- Server
- Management Tools
- Client Connectivity

If SQL Server has been installed somewhere (not necessarily the local machine), select Install Client Tools Option. You need to select the Custom Setup Type. Make sure you install the following subcomponents:

- Full-Text Search on the Select Components page
- Authentication mode on the Select Components page

Note MCMS mixed mode authentication allows connection to an instance of SQL Server using Windows 2000 user account or SQL Server authentication. Using the SQL Server sa login, especially with the No Password option selected, is a known security risk and is not recommended.

- Dictionary order, case-insensitive, for use with the 1252 Character Set on the Collation page

---

Note MCMS 2002 does not support case-sensitive SQL Server names.

- Named Pipes and TCP/IP Sockets on the Network Libraries page.

After you have SQL Server 2000 installed, install SQL Server 2000 SP3. Install the Windows High Security Templates and the MCMS-specific template for the IIS Lockdown Tool.

Task 1-3. Installing High Security Template (hisecws)

Browse to http://go.microsoft.com/fwlink/?LinkId=9558 and install the Windows High Security Template.

Note Windows High Security Template will cause authentication problems on a Windows NT domain controller. Refer to the following Microsoft Knowledge Base articles: "How to Enable SMB Signing in Windows NT" (http://go.microsoft.com/fwlink/?LinkId=9872) and "Cannot Use Shares with LMCompatibilityLevel Set to Only NTLM 2 Authentication" (http://go.microsoft.com/fwlink/?LinkId=9873).

Microsoft recommends installing the IIS Lockdown Tool to provide added security.

Note Refer to "IIS Lockdown Tool" on Microsoft TechNet at http://go.microsoft.com/fwlink/?LinkId=16536.

You must install the IIS Lockdown Tool using instructions specifically for MCMS 2002. The MCMS-customized version of the tool is located on the MCMS CD.

Note Extract the iislockd.exe file as indicated in this procedure. Do not run the executable without extracting the files first.

Task 1-4. Installing the MCMS-Customized Version of the IIS Lockdown Tool

1. Browse to http://go.microsoft.com/fwlink/?LinkId=12340.
2. Download iislockd.exe, save it to your hard drive, and extract the files.
3. Type <path>\iislockd.exe /q /c (full path to where you placed iislockd.exe).
4. Insert the MCMS CD into the drive and navigate to iislockdown.
5. Copy iislockd.ini and urlscan_cms.ini to the folder where the lockdown files were extracted, and then confirm that you want to replace the file.
6. Launch the iislockd.exe file.
7. Select the Content Management Server template (Server Template should be the only template available).
8. Finish the IIS Lockdown Wizard.

> **■Caution** It is recommended that Windows High Security Template (hisecws) be installed before the .NET Framework. If High Security Templates are applied after the .NET Framework, ASPNET_WP user rights will be disabled.

Installing Visual Studio .NET

Visual Studio .NET is the primary development environment for creating MCMS templates and components using the MCMS publishing API. After you've installed Visual Studio .NET, you must install the Microsoft .NET Framework SP2 by running dotnetfxSP2.exe from the Support\Dotnet folder.

Installing Internet Explorer WebControls

To install the Internet Explorer WebControls, run iewebcontrols.msi from the WebControls folder.

Enabling Windows Installer Logging

Microsoft recommends enabling Windows Installer logging before MCMS installation. This creates a log file to use for troubleshooting. If you've never run Windows Installer on your computer, you need to set up a key to enable Windows Installer logging. Local administrator rights are required.

Task 1-5. Setting Up a Key to Enable Windows Installer Logging

1. Launch the Registry Editor.

2. Navigate to HKEY_LOCAL_MACHINE\SOFTWARE\Policies\Microsoft\Windows\ Installer.

3. Add a (String Value) key to the Installer, with the name Logging.

4. Right-click Logging, and then click Modify.

5. Give Logging the value voicewarmup by typing **voicewarmup** in the Value Data box. Click OK and close the Registry Editor.

After logging is enabled, you can check your configuration in the log file. The log file resides in the temp directory. Click Run, type **%temp%** in the Open box, and then click OK.

Creating User Accounts

Two accounts are required on the local Windows 2000 Server (not domain accounts): *MCMS initial administrator* and *MCMS system*. You can use an existing Windows NT user account for the initial MCMS administrator. Microsoft, however, recommends creating a new account for MCMS system.

Initial MCMS Administrator

Initially, an MCMS administrator account must have Create, Edit, and Approve Pages privileges for all containers. The MCMS administrator is the only user who can log on through the Site Manager until other accounts are created. The MCMS administrator must log on to use the Database Configuration Application (DCA) to create or upload a database.

MCMS System Account

MCMS system acts as proxy on behalf of MCMS users to access resources. Microsoft provides the following guidelines for setting up MCMS system:

- If Active Directory is being used, the system account must have view permission to it.

- If the SQL Server database has been configured to use Windows authentication (recommended), the system account must have specific permissions on the SQL Server database.

- Do not set the IIS anonymous account to be the system account.

Note If ASP.NET fails to start because it cannot find a local account named `localmachinename\ASPNET`, you must specify an explicit account in the `<processModel>` section of the `Machine.config` file, or you must use the system account. For more information, see Knowledge Base article Q315158 at `http://go.microsoft.com/fwlink/?LinkId=12910`.

Create an MCMS system account.

Task 1-6. Creating an MCMS System Account

1. Launch the Computer Management service applet in the Administrative Tools group.

2. In the Computer Management window, expand Local Users and Groups; click New User.

3. Enter a user name. The system account can be local; it does not have to be the domain account.

4. Repeat steps 2 and 3 to create a new account for initial MCMS administrator.

5. Click File ➤ Exit.

Creating the MCMS Database and Granting Rights

After the MCMS system account has been configured (MCMS uses MCMS system account credentials to read and write data to the database), you must create the Content Repository—a Microsoft SQL Server database—and grant rights to it. MCMS creates an appropriate database schema and populates it with the required data during the installation process.

■**Note** The SQL Server database contains table definitions and stored procedures that MCMS uses to manage its data store. Information about the structure of a site, content, and resources resides in the database. In MCMS 2002, templates and other page elements have been moved to the file system.

Create a new database.

Task 1-7. Creating a New Database

1. Launch the Enterprise Manager from the Microsoft SQL Server group.

2. Navigate to the Databases folder.

3. Select Add New Database.

4. Name the database using the following conventions:

   • Do not use numbers alone.

   • Use a mixture of letters, numbers, and underscore character.

   • Do not use a Transact-SQL reserved word (SQL Server reserves both uppercase and lowercase versions of reserved words).

Save your changes and use the Console to close the SQL Server Enterprise Manager window or continue with the next procedure to grant MCMS system account rights to the database.

Task 1-8. Granting System Account Rights to the Database

1. Launch the Enterprise Manager from the Microsoft SQL Server group.

2. Expand the Microsoft SQL Servers, and navigate to the server containing the MCMS database.

3. Expand the Security node, Add New Login.

4. Browse to locate the system account user you created previously (use List Names From to select the local computer or domain where you created the system account user).

5. In the Logins pane, select the system account user who will have database access and then open the SQL Server Login Properties dialog box. On the Database Access tab, in the Permit pane, check the box beside the MCMS database that you created. A list of roles appears in the Permit in Database Role; click db_ddladmin, db_datareader, and db_datawriter (db_ddladmin is only needed if you are using the import function in site deployment).

6. Exit SQL Server Enterprise Manager.

You have created a local database and granted MCMS system account rights to that database.

Creating a Web Site for MCMS

You need to create two Web sites: one site for users and content contributors and a second site to act as the entry point for MCMS Server Configuration Application (SCA).

Note When you install IIS with the Common Files, Internet Information Services Snap-In, and World Wide Web Server components, a default Web site is created. Before you add the new MCMS sites, you must provide unique ports for the IIS default site and the two MCMS sites to be created. You should change the TCP port number of the default IIS Web site. Alternatively, add a second IP address to your server and bind each virtual site to a different IP address or simply disable the Default Site option. If you delete the default Web site or if you choose to have MCMS run on another Web site, then you must create that site before installing MCMS. Microsoft recommends creating a separate Web site as the SCA entry point. In Windows 2000 Professional and Windows XP Professional, you can only have one active Web site in IIS, so both the MCMS site and the SCA site will be the same.

Create a new Web site.

Task 1-9. Creating a New Web Site

1. Launch the Computer Management applet from the Administrative Tools group.

2. Expand Services and Applications. Select Create New ➤ Web Site from Internet Information Services. Use the Web Site Creation Wizard to create a new Web site.

3. On the Web Site Description page, type a description.

4. On the IP Address and Port Settings page, type a port number. Microsoft uses 8080 in the tutorials. Do not select a port already used by the IIS Default Web Site or the IIS Administrator Web Site. (Refer to the Windows Help for more information on *ports*.)

5. On the Web Site Home Directory page, click Browse and select a path where you want the home directory to reside. Microsoft uses Local Disk (C:) in the tutorials. If this site is the entry point for the SCA, deselect the Allow Anonymous Access to the Web Site box.

6. On the Web Site Access Permissions page, accept the defaults or select the additional permissions you want to set for the home directory. Finish the wizard.

After a Web site for MCMS has been created, you are ready to install MCMS 2002 Components.

Summary

Unless otherwise stated, for the remainder of this book, we refer to MCMS 2002 operating on Windows Server 2003 or on Windows XP. Many other configurations are possible; however, they will require special configuration. If you want to configure MCMS using one of these alternate configurations, refer to MSDN or TechNet articles or a resource listed in the next section.

Additional Resources

.NET Architecture Center site explains Microsoft's enterprise architecture with key terms, definitions, concept explanations, and helpful illustrations: http://msdn.microsoft.com/architecture/enterprise/default.aspx?pull=/library/en-us/dnea/html/eaarchover.asp

Windows Server System Reference Architecture: http://www.microsoft.com/technet/itsolutions/wssra/default.mspx

TechNet Windows Server 2003 Support site provides a wealth of technical articles and links to Knowledge Base articles. There's a Deployment
Kit, guidelines and recommendations, and an IIS 6.0 Deployment Kit
with "scenario-based guidance" to help you address Web issues:
`http://www.microsoft.com/technet/prodtechnol/windowsserver2003/`
`deployment/default.mspx`

SQL Server requirements: `http://go.microsoft.com/fwlink/`
`?LinkId=16489`

TechNet Support Center for SQL Server 2000 provides downloads for
service packs, best practice guidelines, and a link to the TechNet Virtual
Lab that takes you through testing server deployments without actually
dedicating the resources: `http://www.microsoft.com/technet/prod`➥
`technol/sql/default.mspx`

CHAPTER 2

Configuring MCMS 2002 Components

This chapter covers

- Configuring MCMS 2002 components on a single computer
  - Configuring the MCMS database
  - Configuring the MCMS server
- Configuring MCMS 2002 in a multiple-computer production environment
  - Configuring a multiple-computer production environment
- Installing additional MCMS components
  - Installing Site Manager
  - Installing Site Stager
  - Installing Authoring Connector
  - Activating the Web Author

At this point, you're ready to install Microsoft Content Management Server (with SP1a). You should already have preconfigured your computer with the required software platform; however, if something is missing, it will be detected during setup. The standard Microsoft Setup program is used to install MCMS Content Server, MCMS Developer Tools, MCMS Site Manager, and MCMS Site Stager.

Configuring MCMS 2002 Components on a Single Computer

Figure 2-1 shows the components that will be installed.

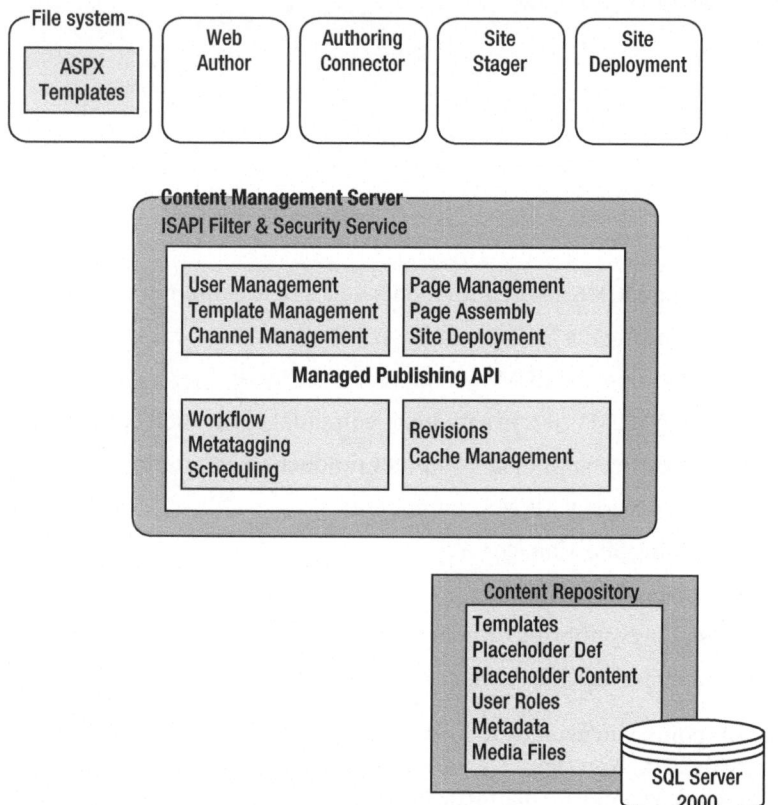

Figure 2-1. *MCMS 2000 components*

Task 2-1. Installing the MCMS Application

When you run the Setup program for MCMS 2002 with SP1a, select CMS Server, Developer Tools, and Site Manager. Leave Site Stager unselected (refer to the Custom Setup page). If you have any concerns about the amount of disk space that will be required, you can deter-mine it at this point.

You can also change the size and location of the cache folder during setup. The default cache location is `<InstallDrive>:\Program Files\Microsoft Content Management ➡ Server\Server`. Further information about the cache will be covered in the Chapter 3.

If desired, leave the Launch Database Configuration Application (DCA) check box selected as you click the Install button. Configuring the database is the next step.

If you're using the original MCMS 2002 CD (without SP1a), or are using the CD/DVD version included with your MSDN Universal Subscription, select only CMS Server during the original installation, with the Launch DCA check box cleared. Install MCMS 2002 SP1A to update the CMS Server. Then use the Control Panel Add/Remove Programs application to "Change" the installation to include MCMS Developer Tools and Site Manager. Leave Site Stager uninstalled.

■**Note** If MCMS 2002 is not installed in the default location, you may experience problems with the WoodgroveNet sample site or other installed Web projects. Refer to the MCMS 2002 Readme file for more details.

The MCMS installation log file is saved in `<InstallDrive>:\Program Files\Micro➡ soft Content Management Server\LogFiles`. If you elected to launch the DCA program, it will start automatically when the MCMS Setup program finishes. If not, the Setup program simply finishes with your acknowledgment.

Configuring the MCMS Database

After the Setup program has completed, the next step is configuring the MCMS Content Repository database using the DCA.

■**Note** To run the DCA, you must have database owner (DBO) privileges. If you are using SQL Server authentication, the SQL Server account you are using must be configured with DBO privileges.

The purpose of the DCA program is to provide connection among the MCMS Web sites (created in the last chapter) and the Content Repository. To complete this task, you must specify the Web site for MCMS Content, specify a Web site for the MCMS SCA, select an MCMS system account, select the MCMS initial Site Manager account, and then finally select and populate your database.

Note If the DCA configuration fails or is cancelled before completion, IIS will restart automatically. If it is installed, you must restart the File Transfer Protocol (FTP) service manually and rerun the DCA to complete the configuration.

If the MCMS DCA did not start automatically when Setup finished, it is located in the Microsoft Content Management Server group in the Start menu structure.

Task 2-2. Configuring the MCMS Database

1. Select the ASP.NET Mode option (choose the MCMS Content Server ASP compatibility mode):

   - **ASP.NET Mode option**: Microsoft recommends this for new sites; it restricts all read-only sites hosted by this MCMS server to ASP.NET-based content. ASP-based content can still be accessed through a read/write site.

   - **Mixed Mode option**: Both *read-only* and *read/write* sites hosted by the MCMS server access ASP-based content. This option provides backward compatibility with MCMS 2001 sites.

2. Select the Web site that will be the primary Web entry point for MCMS (your options appear in the list on the "Select a virtual site for hosting the Microsoft Content Management Server" page):

   - **Web Site selection**: Select the site you created in Chapter 1 to host MCMS content.

   - **Read-Only Site option**: Select to prohibit changes to the MCMS site content.

   - **Read/Write Site option**: Select to enable authoring on the MCMS site.

3. Select the Web entry point for the MCMS Server Configuration Application (SCA Web Entry Point page).

Note A Warning dialog box may appear indicating that you have selected a Web site that is not protected. Addressing security is an important topic for MCMS administration. Refer to Chapter 4 or MSDN for additional information about security.

4. Select the MCMS system account (MCMS System Account page):

   - **User**: The MCMS system account user name requires the following format:
     `<Domain or local machine name>\<username>`

5. If not already granted, grant the logon locally right to the MCMS system account user.

6. Stop the IIS service.

7. From the Select MCMS Database page, select the SQL Server database that will be used as the MSCS Content Repository. The SQL Server Login dialog box is launched with these options:

   - **Server**: Select (local). (We are setting up MCMS on a single computer in this task; after you become familiar with the procedure, you may identify a Content Repository database that is hosted by another MCMS server.) Select Trusted Connection to use Windows Authentication for the SQL database.

   - **Options**: Click Options to expand the SQL Server Login dialog box to view the database.

   - **Database**: Select the SQL Server database you created in a previous task.

8. On the Empty Database dialog box, click Yes to install the MCMS schema into the empty database.

9. Populate the database to initialize the Content Repository data structure. When database population completes, database platform, login, and authentication is confirmed.

10. Select Initial MCMS Administrator:

    - **NT User (Domain\User)**: The Initial MCMS Administrator account name takes the form `<local machine or domain>\<username>`. This account is the only account with access to Site Manager until additional users have been assigned rights.

    - **Password**: Enter the Initial MCMS Administrator password.

    At this point (a Committing Changes page appears briefly), the database is updated with data, and then the MCMS Site Stager Access Confirmation page is displayed.

11. On the DCA MCMS Site Stager Access Confirmation page, select the Yes - Restrict Access to Local Server Machine option.

12. Restart the SQL Server Agent service.

13. Select Launch the SCA to start the Server Configuration Application (SCA) now, or, when ready, start the SCA from the Windows Start menu.

Note If you encountered any issues during the configuration process, you can refer to the log file.

The MCMS Content Server is now installed on one computer. The next step is configuring the MCMS Content Server using the MCMS SCA.

Note Microsoft also recommends installing the WoodgroveNet sample site for testing purposes. The sample site is included on the product CD.

Configuring the MCMS Server

You must configure the MCMS server by assigning Windows user accounts on the MCMS server to MCMS rights groups. MCMS rights groups control the access of users to the MCMS applications and sites.

The MCMS SCA utility is used to configure the MCMS server (or multiple servers). After a new installation, users can selectively configure—globally or on just one server—activities such as changing the MCMS 2002 system account, adding and removing supported Windows NT domains, and adding or removing Active Directory groups as the network topology changes or grows.

For additional information about adding users to rights groups, see the topic "Using the Server Configuration Application" in MCMS 2002 Help.

Task 2-3. Configuring MCMS Server

1. If the SCA did not start automatically when you completed the database configuration, launch it from the Microsoft Content Management Server group.

2. Note the version information for MCMS 2002 with SP1a, as well as the database name, and server information.

3. Review the other tabs for future reference.

4. Click the Access tab in the MCMS Configuration Application window. If your local machine name is not listed, click Configure. Type in the machine name and click Add to add it to the list of supported Windows NT domains.

5. Close the SCA.

Configuring MCMS 2002 in a Multiple-Computer Production Environment

A high-volume production environment consists of not only multiple computers but also multiple developers. Figure 2-2 shows the options that you may need to implement when installing MCMS 2002 in such an environment: Development server, Content Authoring server, Site Staging server, and Production servers.

Figure 2-2 shows a server to support each of the MCMS functions: a development server for creating and testing the code base, a primary content authoring server that maintains the up-to-date content, a staging server to handle replication and staging (converting to static HTML), and production servers. The production environment includes a server for reading/writing, a production server to provide dynamic content, and one for

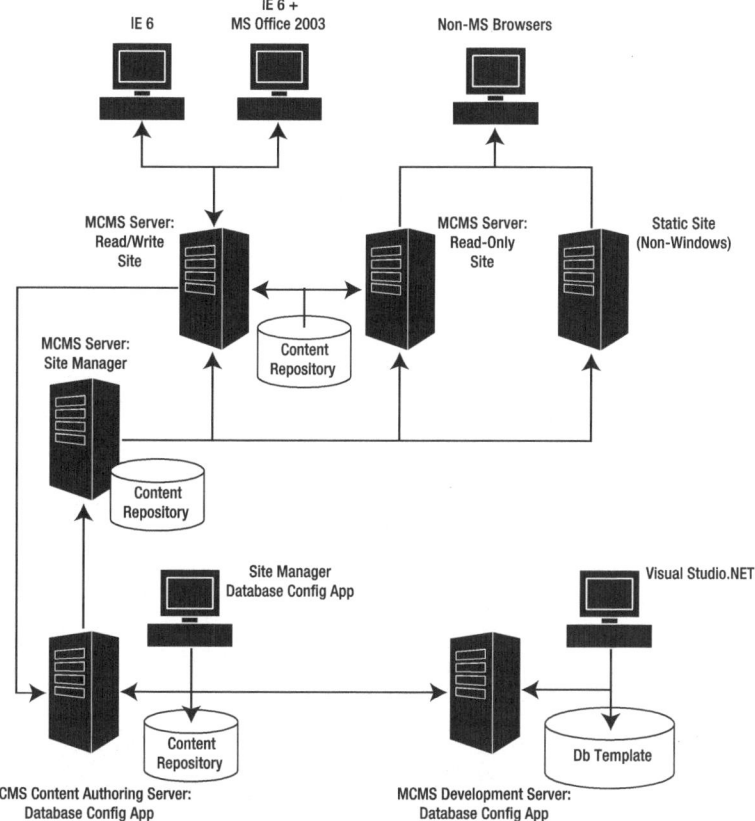

Figure 2-2. *MCMS server functions*

static content. Depending upon the load or requirements of the site, you can merge functions in the same server or add additional server resources where the load is heaviest.

For more information about multiple developers, refer to "Setting Up a Multideveloper Environment" in MCMS 2002 Help.

Configuring a Multiple-Computer Production Environment

To install MCMS 2002 on multiple computers in a production or testing environment, you must preconfigure individual computers as described in Chapter 1. Logging should be enabled on all computers targeted for MCMS component installation.

Similar to a single-system configuration, tasks must be completed in the order in which they are listed here:

1. Create the MCMS database and grant rights.

2. Create the MCMS Web site.

3. Install Content Server.

4. Configure the MCMS database in a multiple-computer setup.

5. Install Site Manager.

Granting Rights to the MCMS Database

After you have installed the prerequisite platform software as described in Chapter 1, you need to create the Content Repository database. (Recall, MCMS uses the Content Repository to store content. MCMS creates the appropriate database schema and populates it with the required data during the installation process.) This preconfiguration procedure is identical whether performed in a single- or multiple-computer environment (refer to Chapter 1). After the MCMS 2002 Content Repository (a SQL Server database) is created, rights must be granted to it.

The MCMS Content Server uses the MCMS system account credentials to read and write data to the database.

Task 2-4. Granting Rights to the Database for the MCMS System Account

1. On the MCMS Server computer, launch the Enterprise Manager from the Microsoft SQL Server group.

2. Expand the Microsoft SQL Servers node, and then navigate to the server containing the MCMS database.

3. Expand the Security node, and click Logins.

4. Browse to locate the system account user you created previously in the Name section of the New Login dialog box.

5. Select the domain where you created the system account user from the List Names From pane. Add the system account user (from the Names pane), confirm your selection, and then close the New Login dialog box.

6. Select the system account user who will have access to the database in the Logins pane. Open the SQL Server Login Properties dialog box. Check the box beside the MCMS database that you created on the Permit pane of the Database Access tab.

   A list of roles is displayed in the Permit in Database Role pane.

7. Select db_datareader, db_datawriter, and db_ddladmin from the Permit in Database Role pane and confirm your selections. (db_ddladmin permission is needed only if site deployment uses the import function.)

8. Exit the Console (SQL Server Enterprise Manager).

You have now granted rights for the MCMS system account to the Content Repository. Next, you'll create the Web site for MCMS.

Creating a Web Site for MCMS

As with a single-computer configuration, you need two Web sites for MCMS: one site for MCMS and a second site to serve as the entry point for the MCMS SCA.

When you install IIS with the Common Files, Internet Information Services Snap-In, and World Wide Web Server components, a default Web site is created. If you delete the default Web site or if you choose to have MCMS run on another Web site, then you must create a site before installing MCMS. Microsoft recommends you create a separate Web site as the SCA entry point.

Note Refer to Windows 2000 Professional and Windows XP Professional Help for more information about creating Web sites using IIS.

Task 2-5. Creating a New Web Site

1. Launch the Computer Management applet in the Administrative Tools group.

2. Expand Services and Applications.

3 Navigate to the Internet Information Services; right-click and select the Web Site Creation Wizard to create a new Web site.

3. On the Web Site Description page, type a description; for example, Microsoft uses "SCA Entry Point" in the tutorials.

4. On the IP Address and Port Settings page, type a port number. Microsoft uses 8080 in the tutorials. (Do not select a port already used by the IIS Default Web site or the IIS Administrator Web site.)

   Refer to the Windows Help for more information on ports.

5. Browse and select the path where you want the home directory to reside (Web Site Home Directory page); if this site is the entry point for the SCA, deselect the Allow Anonymous Access to the Web Site check box.

6. Accept the defaults or select the additional permissions on the Web Site Access Permissions page. Finish the wizard.

After you have created a Web site for MCMS, you're ready to install MCMS 2002 components.

Setting Up a Multideveloper Environment

In general, it takes a variety of developers to build a MCMS 2002 Web site. Follow these guidelines to configure a multideveloper environment:

- Install MCMS on each developer's computer. Add Microsoft Visual Studio .NET and a source control client, such as Microsoft Visual SourceSafe.

- Provide a shared MCMS Content Repository (SQL Server database) for all developer MCMS systems to use. Make sure the shared system provides check-in and check-out functionality on the database.

- Provide a shared test-bed MCMS server, which is also connected to the shared MCMS Content Repository. A staging or test environment is typically part of the overall environment. At a well-defined point in time, the MCMS Content Repository that the developers use is deployed to the test environment, as well as the latest versions of the file-based assets and the IIS infrastructure, such as virtual directories.

Note MCMS provides functionality to deploy the MCMS Content Repository from one server to one or more other servers. You can use Microsoft Application Center to deploy the file-based and IIS infrastructure assets of the Web site.

Installing Microsoft Content Management Server

Install MCMS Content Server on your public Web server and your Web Authoring server. Content Server responds to page requests by dynamically assembling Web pages from components in the Content Repository (database) and templates file system.

The Web Authoring server provides access to postings for those who have author permission. On the author's system, only Internet Explorer 5.5 or later is required. Content is submitted using the MCMS Web Author, which is provided by the Web Authoring Content Server.

Note For additional information about adding users to rights groups, see the topic "Using the Server Configuration Application" in MCMS 2002 Help.

Task 2-6. Installing MCMS Content Server

1. On the computer that will run MCMS Content Server, launch the MCMS 2002 setup program.

2. On the Custom Setup page, select only CMS Server.

3. On the Customer Information page, enter the user name for your administrator account in the following form: `<local machine or domain>\<username>`.

More information is available in Chapter 3 on changing the default disk cache folder location and cache size.

The Database Configuration Application opens after you install Content Server.

Configuring the MCMS Database in a Multiple-Computer Setup

In this step, you will be configuring a multicomputer environment, such as you would create for a production environment. The same issues must be addressed: you select and populate your database, select a MCMS system account and the initial Site Manager account, and specify the virtual Web site for MCMS. This time, however, they need to be configured with the understanding that not all components reside on every computer.

As in the single-computer environment, the user running the DCA must have database owner (DBO) privileges on the database.

▪Note If the DCA did not start automatically when Setup completed, launch it manually. It is located in the Microsoft Content Management Server group.

Task 2-7. Configuring the MCMS Database

1. Select the ASP option (choose the MCMS Content Server ASP compatibility mode):

   - **ASP.NET Mode**: Microsoft recommends this for new sites; it restricts all read-only sites hosted by this MCMS server to ASP.NET-based content. ASP-based content can still be accessed through a read/write site.

   - **Mixed Mode**: Both read-only and read/write sites hosted by the MCMS server access ASP-based content. This option provides backward compatibility with MCMS 2001 sites.

2. Select the Web site that will be the primary Web entry point for MCMS (your options appear in the list on the "Select a virtual site for hosting the Microsoft Content Management Server" page):

- **Default Web Site**: Specifies the default Web site as the primary Web entry point for MCMS.
- **Read/Write Site**: Enables authoring on the MCMS site.

  If you created a different MCMS site (Chapter 1), you can select it here.

3. Select the Web entry point for SCA on the SCA Web Entry Point page.

Note If a Warning dialog box appears, you have selected a Web site that is not protected. Addressing security is an important topic for MCMS administration. Refer to Chapter 4 or the MSDN for additional information about security.

---

4. Select the MCMS system account on the MCMS System Account page:
   - **User**: The MCMS system account user must be the local computer name `<local machine>\<username>`.

5. Stop the IIS service.

6. Select the database that will be used as the Content Repository on the Select MCMS Database page. The SQL Server Login dialog box is launched containing the following options:
   - **Server**: Select local to identify a database on the local computer or navigate to a remote (hosted by another MCMS server) database.
   - **Options**: Click Options to expand the SQL Server Login dialog box to view the database.
   - **Database**: Select the database you created.

7. In the Empty Database dialog box, click Yes.

8. Populate the database to initialize the Content Repository data structure. When database population completes, database platform, login, and authentication is confirmed.

9. Select Initial MCMS Administrator:
   - **NT User (Domain\User)**: The initial MCMS administrator account name takes the form `<local machine or domain>\<username>`. This account is the only account with access to Site Manager until additional users have been assigned rights.

   At the Committing Changes page, the database is updated with data, and then the MCMS Site Stager Access Confirmation page appears.

10. On the MCMS Site Stager Access Confirmation page, select Restrict Access to Local Server Machine.

11. [Optional] Select Launch the SCA to start the SCA.

■**Note** If you encountered any issues during the configuration process, you can refer to the log file.

The MCMS server is now installed. You still have some configuration left to do before the site is operational, and you will need to install the Authoring Connector if you want authors to work with Microsoft Office.

■**Note** Microsoft recommends installing the WoodgroveNet sample site for test purposes. The sample site is included on the product CD.

Installing Site Manager

MCMS Site Manager can be installed on either a server or client computer, or on multiple computers. MCMS Site Manager requires Windows 2000 Professional with SP2 or higher (SP3 or higher is recommended), Windows 2000 Server with SP2 or higher, Windows 2000 Advanced Server with SP2 or higher, or Windows XP Professional with SP1 or higher.

Task 2-8. Installing Procedures

1. Run the MCMS 2002 Setup on all computers that will run MCMS Site Manager.

2. To install only MCMS Site Manager, clear all components except Site Manager on the Custom Setup page.

Installing Additional MCMS Components

In this section, we'll cover installing additional MCMS components that don't necessarily run on the MCMS server: the Site Manager, Site Stager, and the MCMS 2002 Authoring Connector (a wizard-based application). We'll also cover activating the MCMS Web Author on a client computer, which is actually not an install, just an automated download of an ActiveX control.

■**Note** For additional information on using MCMS 2002 Authoring Connector Help, refer to "Viewing MCMS 2002 Documentation" in the MSDN library.

Installing Site Manager

You can install MCMS Site Manager on either a server or a client computer. Perform a Custom Install using the MCMS 2002 (SP1a) CD.

Task 2-9. Installing Site Manager (Only)

1. Use Add/Remove Programs on the Control Panel and launch the MCMS 2002 setup program.
2. During the installation process, select Custom installation.
3. Clear all selections except Site Manager.
4. Complete the installation.

■**Note** If you upgraded (for example, MCMS or MCMS 2002 with SP1 to MCMS 2002 with SP1a), all MCMS components are removed; however, the system will not revert to a previously installed version. Any MCMS files, regardless of whether they've been modified directly, are removed; however, if new files have been added to MCMS directories, Uninstall does not remove them, but instead deletes the virtual mappings created in MCMS. Any database changes that you made after the initial configuration remain intact.

Installing Site Stager

You can install MCMS Site Stager on either the source or destination computer. Microsoft recommends installing it on the destination computer and letting it "pull down" a new staged site as required. This process can also be automated at the source computer.

■**Note** If you followed the Microsoft recommendations when you installed MCMS 2002, you chose ASP.NET as the operation mode. Currently, Site Stager will not stage an ASP.NET site; however, by the time you read this, Microsoft may have issued a service patch to remedy this problem.

Task 2-10. Installing Site Stager (Only)

1. Use Add/Remove Programs on the Control Panel and launch the MCMS 2002 setup program.

2. During the installation process, select Custom installation.

3. Clear all selections except Site Stager.

4. Complete the installation.

■Note If you upgraded (for example, MCMS or MCMS 2002 with SP1 to MCMS 2002 with SP1a), all MCMS components are removed; however, the system will not revert to a previously installed version. Any MCMS files, regardless of whether they've been modified directly, are removed; however, if new files have been added to MCMS directories, Uninstall does not remove them, but instead deletes the virtual mappings created in MCMS. Any database changes that you made after the initial configuration remain intact.

Installing Authoring Connector

The MCMS Authoring Connector is not typically installed on the server, but instead is installed on a client computer for a user (author) with the appropriate rights to add content to the CMS Web site. The client computer must first meet the following requirements:

• Windows XP Professional with SP1 or higher, Windows 2000 Professional with SP2 or higher, Windows 2000 Server with SP2 or higher, or Windows 2000 Advanced Server with SP2 or higher

• Word XP or Word 2003

• Internet Explorer 6.0 or later

When you install the Authoring Connector, you will identify the author for whom the software is being installed, as well as the CMS server to which the Author Connector will be connected.

Task 2-11. Installing the Authoring Connector

1. Insert the MCMS 2002 CD with SP1a into the CD-ROM drive of the client computer.

2. On the MCMS splash screens, select Install Components and then Install Authoring Connector.

3. On the Customer Information page, enter your user name and company. Also select the option to allow only you, or to allow anyone using this computer, to use the Authoring Connector.

4. On the Choose Destination Location page, either accept the default location or enter an alternate location.

5. On the Choose Server page, either accept the default server (machine name) or select a different MCMS server.

Activating the Web Author

Users can use the Authoring Connector or author directly from the Web site using MCMS Web Author. Web Author requires Internet Explorer 5.5 or later. To use the Web Author, a client computer must download an ActiveX control containing the product.

To activate the Web Author, the Read/Write Site option must have been selected during the MCMS installation.

Task 2-12. Activating the Web Author

1. Navigate to the Web site on which you want to perform author functions, and log on.

2. The ActiveX control is automatically updated on your computer and the Web Author is now available for use.

Note MCMS 2002 Help is installed only on the server and with MCMS 2002 Site Manager. Authoring Connector and Web Author users must access the documentation directly from the CD. For additional information, refer to the MCMS 2002 Help system topic "Viewing MCMS 2002 Documentation."

Summary

In this chapter, we've covered configuring MCMS 2002 components on single- and multiple-computer production environments. Obviously, there are many configurations we haven't covered, but this chapter provided the basic guidelines for setting up production and development environments to suit most applications. The MCMS user base is growing and best-practice guidelines are becoming available on the MSDN site. You might also want to check out two other references if your installation is a bit off the beaten path: *Microsoft Content Management Server 2002: A Complete Guide* (Addison-Wesley Professional, 2004) and *Building Web Sites with MCMS* (Packt Publishing, 2004).

As mentioned before, MCMS is a powerful tool and there are many business scenarios where MCMS will provide significant efficiencies right out of the box; however, MCMS is a "solutions" tool. Expect to do some significant programming to tailor your site to your needs.

■ ■ ■

CHAPTER 3

Measuring and Tuning Performance

This chapter covers

- Performance optimization
  - Caching
  - Balancing items in containers
  - Using API searches efficiently
  - Limiting the use of placeholders
  - Site navigation considerations
- Capacity planning
  - Analysis and general considerations
  - Transactions
  - Failure of criteria
  - Building a test site

Microsoft Content Management Server provides tools to plan, analyze, and test an MCMS Web site to optimize its performance and ensure that it can meet the required load. Optimal performance is achieved through optimization of caching, scaling, and tuning to eliminate throughput bottlenecks.

Data provided in this section have been compiled from tests and analyses that Microsoft has performed using the Microsoft Web Application Stress Tool (WAST) and the Transaction Cost Analysis (TCA) tool from the Microsoft Commerce Server 2000 performance toolkit. WAST is a load-generation tool and TCA acts as a WAST controller. This chapter presents Microsoft's recommendations for MCMS settings (primarily caching) that can be tuned to increase site performance and ameliorate known performance limitations. This chapter also covers site design considerations and capacity planning at a high level.

Performance Optimization

Optimal performance is primarily based on the speed at which a page is served. Testing performance, therefore, requires projecting requests per second. Throughput is measured as

- **Pages per second**: A page is what the user sees after making a request; one page can contain many data (ASP) requests that a server must execute or redirect.

- **ASP requests per second**: Each ASP request can contain many Get requests.

- **Gets per second**: Individual requests for objects such as images.

The number of concurrent users on the site also affects throughput. Two methods to maximize performance seem to yield useful results:

- Tuning performance with configuration settings and fragment caching

- Careful planning of site content at designtime, such as containers, searches, placeholders, and navigation

Caching

Microsoft recommends setting the system cache to a size large enough to hold the bulk of your binary data. Make sure the maximum number of nodes in the memory cache is sufficient to hold the most commonly accessed pages on your site. Keep in mind that a single page may require many nodes to be displayed, depending on such elements as navigation, page depth, and siblings. Performance of Web entry points marked as read-only can also improve 10% on average (MCMS uses less script code to serve a read-only request than read/write). Read-only and read/write entry points for the same site may require different-sized caches.

Object retrieval directly from the Content Repository for every transaction often presents a bottleneck. To improve response time, MCMS provides memory-object and file-system (disk) caches. The memory object cache stores data relating to API objects (channels, placeholders, and so on) and is queried when an object is requested. The file system cache stores binary data—resources, such as graphics and templates.

Each page request requires rendering a number of COM objects (into HTML), and each time, the objects are created and destroyed. Fragment caching saves the output obtained from the first rendering into the cache. The fragment is output immediately and is stored in the cache for future use, with little overhead. Use fragment caching for guest access because it's typically the most frequent during high loads. Fragment caching should not be used during site design because new objects are constantly being created, which causes the cache to flush. Also, because the number of concurrent users designing site elements is usually lower than at runtime, there is little to be gained. Fragment caching can also conflict with authenticated access.

Set Disk Cache Location

Use the MCMS SCA to set cache location by entering the location or navigating to the directory for the local disk cache.

Note The SCA does not allow you to specify a different drive.

Task 3-1. Setting Cache Location

1. Launch the SCA (Content Management Server 2002 group). Select the Cache tab, and then click Configure.

2. To set Local Disk Cache Location, type or browse to navigate to a directory.

3. Close the SCA.

Set Maximum Cache Size

Set the maximum size of the cache in megabytes (MB) using the SCA.

Task 3-2. Setting Cache Size

1. Launch the SCA, select the Cache tab, and click Configure.

2. In the Maximum Disk Cache Size section:

   - **Use Global Default**: Use global maximum cache size.
   - **Set Global**: Set maximum global cache size.
   - **Use Local Override:** Use the local setting for maximum cache size.
   - **Current Override Value**: Set local maximum cache size.

3. In the Maximum Nodes in Memory Cache section:

   - **Use Global Default**: Use the global value for maximum number of nodes.
   - **Set Global**: Set the global maximum number of nodes.
   - **Use Local Override**: Use local setting for maximum number of nodes.
   - **Current Override Value**: Enter local value for maximum number of nodes.

4. Save settings and close the SCA.

Clear Memory Cache

Clear the memory cache to remove temporary files stored in memory.

Task 3-3. Clearing Memory Cache

1. Launch the SCA, select the Cache tab, and click Clear Memory Cache.

2. Click OK to clear the cache and close the SCA.

Balancing Items in Containers

If the number of items in any one container is too high, performance is degraded (accessing a container instantiates all items in the container). Although the maximum number is hardware dependent, Microsoft recommends a maximum of 400 items per container. Distribute items over multiple containers and you won't exceed the maximum. The greater the number of items, the more impact fragment caching has.

Using API Searches Efficiently

API searches may query the database, which may be loading the database. If searching is slow, use SQL Server Query Analyzer to see how the database is loaded during searches. Use searches sparingly and make use of fragment caching. Use SQL Server Query Analyzer to monitor the database load and query execution.

■**Note** For additional information about SQL Server Query Analyzer, refer to the MSDN article at http://msdn.microsoft.com/library/default.asp?url=/library/ en-us/qryanlzr/qryanlzr_1zqq.asp.

Limiting the Use of Placeholders

A clear rule of thumb about response time is the more placeholders per page, the longer the processing time. Placeholder collections are treated like other MCMS collections (instantiates all placeholders per page).

■**Note** Best practice: Do not store metadata in a placeholder; instead, use custom properties.

Site Navigation Considerations

One important feature of MCMS is dynamic navigation. MCMS generates a page-centric navigation bar—a context-sensitive set of navigation links from the rendered page to those around it. On frameless sites, dynamic navigation is generated for every page request. Dynamic navigation is costly because it touches many objects. If navigation is deep, performance will be adversely affected.

> ▓**Note** Best practice: To help offset this overload, use fragment caching.

Capacity Planning

The goal of capacity planning is to implement an installation that can handle your site's projected load. What is the business goal that you are trying to achieve? What are users going to request and how many will visit the site? What latency, in terms of response time, is acceptable? How many contributors will be submitting content and under what conditions?

When you have finished your analysis, you should have the following tasks completed:

- Map the workflow of your personnel to MCMS publishing workflow.

- Identify managerial, authoring, administrative, development, design, review, and editorial roles.

- Assign development roles (moderator, resource manager, and template designer).

- Define the automated publishing process (development, content contribution, staging, testing, and production).

Don't forget, administrators and content managers require training. MCMS 2002 administrative and user tutorials are available in the MCMS 2002 documentation.

Capacity planning is also a dynamic activity; after your site is operational, monitoring performance helps you adjust to actual demand. In this subsection, we'll go over a capacity planning strategy that includes considering initial guidelines, testing the installation's response to load, and making long-term projections.

Analysis and General Guidelines

Optimal performance of the MCMS installation depends on the Web server's and database server's disk speed, RAM, and so on, as well as the general throughput of the network connection. However, some logical areas need examination as well:

- Runtime production server load
- Authentication
- Content contribution load (mix of designtime and runtime operations)
- Deployment options

Use the following list of general guidelines when determining capacity planning for your site:

- Read-only sites are restricted to the Web server CPU; dynamic sites can create loads on the local server and other servers that resolve placeholders with content from the repository.
- Authoring makes up a very small percentage of a site's traffic, even in large sites.
- Deployments are database-, CPU-, and Web Server CPU–intensive.

Transactions

A clear understanding of planned targets is invaluable in creating a set of transaction goals:

- Determine the business issue being addressed with this site.
- Talk to employees from different levels in the management hierarchy about their job functions and departmental growth projections.
- Validate and compare your estimates against other industry figures or other sites your company operates.
- Determine the anticipated user base.
- Review known industry results and traffic levels.
- For e-commerce sites, determine browse-to-buy and hits-before-purchase ratios.
- Determine peak traffic volumes—what is the range between average and peak traffic?

In your analysis of site requirements, you must first determine the type of business that is being transacted. Follow-up questions will be easier to tailor and, based on the results, estimating capacity requirements will be more accurate.

Let's take a quick look at a few metrics for which Microsoft has provided some analysis.

Pages per Second

If you are analyzing an e-commerce site, your company will have developed a business plan with some metrics such as site revenue, average sale, browse-to-buy ratio, average number of pages per visit, and so on:

- $50 million in revenue through the site
- Average customer sale $40
- Expected browse-to-buy ratio 1.3%
- Average user visits 10 pages

Microsoft provides a formula to estimate the throughput:

```
((revenue / avg sales / browse to buy ratio) _ avg pages visited
× requests per page) / secs
```

Plugging in the numbers

```
((50,000,000 / 40 / .013) _ 10 _ 3)/Second per year = ~95 pages/sec
```

yields a page throughput in number of pages per second that you can test against.

Number of Users

Again Microsoft provides some analysis fine points that can be addressed for efficiency's sake. Estimating the number of concurrent users requires examining the following:

- How long will users browse?
- What constitutes the maximum load? Average versus peak loads? Will day/dates, times, and special events or offers (holiday shopping) drive the maximum load?
- What is the registered user base? The projected growth rate?

To calculate concurrent load, follow these steps:

1. Calculate the number of requests at peak using the formula

   ```
   Visitors × requests × peak / seconds in a day
   ```

2. Calculate the maximum concurrent users using the formula

   ```
   Visitors × length × peak / minutes per day
   ```

3. Compare how much greater peak is than average.

Page Size

User *walk-away* happens when response time grows too long. Microsoft suggests a good rule of thumb is that pages serve up in less than 5 seconds. Large pages tend to be slow to serve up. Graphics and placeholders are the primary cause of MCMS pages becoming too large.

Microsoft offers the following table (see Table 3-1) comparing page size and response time for typical connection speeds. Remember, walk-away becomes a factor at around a 5-second response latency.

Table 3-1. *Page Size and Response Time*

Access Type	Throughput	2KB	10KB	20KB	50KB	100KB	1MB
28.8K	28800	0.6	2.8	5.7	14.2	28.4	291.3
56K	57600	0.3	1.4	2.8	7.1	14.2	145.6
DSL	640000	0.0	0.1	0.3	0.6	1.3	13.1
Cable modem	800000	0.0	0.1	0.2	0.5	1.0	10.5

Bandwidth

Bandwidth is clearly a key decision. Microsoft suggests that a site with a peak load of 163 page requests per second serving an average page size of 30KB will require 38Mbps at peak load.

Failure Criteria

Failure criteria can be determined based on a variety of factors. Typically, however, failure occurs when the MCMS server's CPU load exceeds 85%. (It's arbitrary, but at 85%, Microsoft suggests that further throughput is not likely.) When latency becomes exceedingly high, be vigilant. Latency creeps up slowly until a sudden sharp increase alerts you that you have reached the point of overstress.

Note It is important not to measure throughput after the failure point has been reached.

In general, throughput should be measured at the point just prior to failure criteria being met or when latency is less than 5 seconds, whichever occurs first. Depending on your configuration, other resources such as memory consumed, disk I/O, or network bandwidth might be identified as the performance-limiting factor.

Building a Test Site

Empirical data are required to tune performance optimally and plan capacity accurately. After you have made your capacity estimates, test them on a non-production site. Based on the data you acquire about users and loads, develop a usage profile. Use the tools provided by MCMS to slowly increase loading until the failure criteria are met.

Note Watch for other system bottlenecks that prevent failure criteria from being reached.

Keep in mind that different sites have different performance characteristics. Measure performance early, often, and throughout the life cycle of a site. Key performance counters you should monitor include

- ASP/sec

- SQL monitoring

- % CPU (Web server and database server)

- Memory usage (especially with deployment)

    For latency measurement note:

- Time to last byte (TTLB), which means how much time to process and download

- Time to first byte (TTFB), which means how much time spent processing a page

- ASP request execution time

- ASP errors/sec (there should not be any)

- Requests queued, requests waiting, and ASP request wait time, which are useful for determining if there is an overstress situation

MCMS provides a set of test tools you can use to make throughput calculations easier and more accurate. Two of the tools are the Transaction Cost Analysis tool and the Web Application Stress Tool.

Transaction Cost Analysis (TCA) Tool

The TCA tool, which calculates the amount of hardware required to support a given number of users, is an ideal tool to use for your throughput analysis. TCA simplifies transaction cost analysis and allows you to draw a bead on the cost of operation.

TCA is used in conjunction with the WAST to develop loading scenarios and then analyze the throughput costs.

Web Application Stress Tool (WAST)

WAST allows you to stress test. You record scripts that make requests and build a list of URLs to simulate user transactions. The WAST applies successively more load until failure occurs. TCA operates as a WAST driver to automate testing. With the TCA/WAST test bed, a site planner now has a procedure for incrementally increasing the system load and monitoring performance counters. The WAST/TCA test bed will also terminate a test when a specific failure criterion is reached. TCA produces Excel graphs of measured performance counters and calculates the cost of user transactions.

TCA performed in this way allows you to project the number of concurrent users your site can handle given specific hardware constraints. In short, you determine current capacity, identify options for improvement, and determine areas where scale is a viable solution.

TCA Testing Guidelines: Document Your Site

To create test scripts that will reflect your site's usage pattern, you need to document the details of your site as follows.

Document site details:

- Hardware
  - Diagrams network topology: firewalls, network speed of transfer between hardware
  - Hardware resource metrics: CPU speed, memory, and so on
- Software
  - Versions, service packs, hot fixes
- Site complexity
  - Number of pages and channels in the site
  - Placeholders/page, containers with large number of items
  - API searches
  - Dynamic navigation/fragment caching

The more a test environment parallels the actual production environment, the more accurate the results.

TCA Testing Guidelines: Determine User Profile

To obtain a useful throughput measurement, you must test the site in a condition that reflects how users will access the site (which pages, frequency, and concurrency). A user profile for an existing site can be created by the following:

- Analyzing IIS traffic logs
- Accessing Commerce Server 2000 analytics
- Using third-party log tools

It's not as easy if the site is new. Because no data exists, you must rely on estimates; however, these data need to be validated with a test bed. Data to be acquired include

- Average session length
- Average number of operations performed in a session
- Most frequently visited pages
- Hit statistics for most frequently visited pages
- Difference between average and peak loads

Prototypical user profile data is shown in Table 3-2. (These data were obtained from the Performance Optimization and Capacity Planning sections of MCMS documentation. They were developed from IIS log files.) The user profile tabulated here is based on 11 operations in an 11-minute session (1 minute think time between operations).

Table 3-2. *User Profile Data*

User Transaction	Page Hits	Hit Ratio %	Operations
Home page	58,285	22.82	2.5
Search (good)	36,641	14.35	1.6
Search (bad)	2,599	1.02	0.1
Add item	4,482	1.76	0.2
Add item + delete	2,726	1.07	0.1
Add item + checkout	2,800	1.10	0.1
Browse	93,507	36.61	4.0
Login	4,418	1.73	0.2
Register	2,700	1.06	0.1
Zip code	40,771	15.96	1.8
View cart	6,452	2.53	0.3
Totals	255,381	100.00	11.0

Typically 10% of the total number of pages account for 90% of the traffic. Create usage profiles for both development and production servers. Use the development profile to determine the amount of content to be deployed and frequency. Factor replication loads into both production and development servers.

■**Tip**   Generally, only a few operations comprise 95% of usage.

■**Note**   If your site will serve multiple audiences or will be employed to address different scenarios, varying performance characteristics may arise for each usage scenario. A separate TCA should be run for each usage profile.

Create Stress Scripts

The WAST allows you to automate the stress testing based on the usage profiles that you identified previously.

To create one script for each operation, follow these steps:

1. Configure WAST to record performance counter data. Refer to the list of performance metrics outlined previously in the "Building a Test Site" section.

2. Configure the TCA tool to execute WAST scripts for each operation (slowly increasing the load until failure).

3. Record the maximum throughput obtained just before failure. Also note the percentage use of the failure counter at this point.

4. Calculate the cost of each operation using the formula

   ```
   (% Utilization _ Total Power) / Throughput = Cost per operation
   ```

■**Caution**   Watch for other system bottlenecks that prevent failure criteria from being reached.

■**Note**   Scripts are run without think time.

> ▦**Note** If CPU is the performance-limiting resource, the Excel graphs created from TCA will calculate the cost per operation for you.

Cost per User

After usage profiles are determined and the cost of each operation is established, the cost per user operation per second can be calculated (see Table 3-3). Microsoft has provided data for the prototypical operations identified in the example profile you saw earlier in Table 3-2.

Table 3-3. *Cost per User Operation per Second*

Operations	Hit Ratio	UPOs*	UPOs per Sec**	Cost per Op (Mcycles)	Cost per User Op per Sec***
Home page	22.82	2.5	0.003804	53.77	0.2045
Search (good)	14.35	1.6	0.002391	150.12	0.3590
Search (bad)	1.02	0.1	0.000170	42.08	0.0071
Add item	1.76	0.2	0.000293	261.54	0.0765
Add item + delete	1.07	0.1	0.000178	359.56	0.0640
Add item + checkout	1.10	0.1	0.000183	415.22	0.0759
Browse	36.61	4.0	0.006102	58.50	0.3570
Login	1.73	0.2	0.000288	251.69	0.0726
Register	1.06	0.1	0.000176	62.39	0.0110
Zip code	15.96	1.8	0.002661	70.10	0.1865
View cart	2.53	0.3	0.000421	84.50	0.0356
Totals		11.0			1.4496

* *(over 11 min, 660 sec)*
** *(UPO/660 sec)*
*** *(Cost per op * UPO/sec)*

The cost per user operation per second for each operation in the profile can be added together to find the total cost per second of a user on the site.

Capacity

Calculate projected capacity using this formula:

```
Users × Cost per user
```

Using the cost per user calculated previously (1.4496 CPU cycles), Table 3-4 shows results for a gradually increasing number of users.

Table 3-4. *Gradually Increasing Numbers of Users*

Users	Cost (Mcycles)
0	0.0
50	72.5
100	145.0
150	217.5
200	290.0
250	362.5
300	435.0
400	580.0
450	652.5
500	725.0
550	797.5
600	870.0

Finally, to calculate capacity based on CPU usage (%) and the cost per user, use this formula:

```
Capacity = CPU budget/User Profile Cost
```

This formula allows you to estimate the number of users that can be supported for any specific CPU use percentage.

```
User Capacity @ 50% CPU = 400 Mcycles/1.4496 = 276 users
User Capacity @ 75% CPU = 600 Mcycles/1.4496 = 414 users
```

Summary

Become familiar with business requirements, goals, and growth projections. Determine the user base and the transactions that will occur. Create usage profiles that reflect the actual page requests and operations that will take place after the site is operating at full capacity. Examine page size and reduce the use of graphics and placeholders to minimize latency for page turnaround. Consider your site's bandwidth requirements. After you have a clear estimate of site usage, build a test bed that parallels the actual usage scenario(s). Use the MCMS TCA and the WAST to stress test your test site. Calculate the cost per user in CPU cycles and from that determine the hardware required to support the numbers of users you expect.

Additional Resources

Best Practices: Developing Solutions Using the Content Management Server 2002 Connector for SharePoint Technologies. `http://msdn.` `microsoft.com/library/default.asp?url=/library/en-us/dnmscms02/` `html/mscms_CMS02FAQ.asp`

TechNet article "Capacity Model for Internet Transactions" covers minimizing the total dollar cost of ownership, transaction supporting throughput targets, and maintaining acceptable response-times: `http://www.microsoft.com/technet/prodtechnol/comm/comm2002/` `plan/capmodit.mspx`

Transcript for Microsoft Support WebCast: Performance Tuning in Microsoft Content Management Server 2002: `http://support.` `microsoft.com/default.aspx?scid=%2Fservicedesks%2F`➥ `webcasts%2Fen%2Ftranscripts%2Fwct121603.asp`

CHAPTER 4

■ ■ ■

Authentication

This chapter covers

- Windows accounts
- Forms-based authentication using IIS
    - Anonymous user access
    - Secure Sockets Layer (SSL)
    - Logon page
    - Web.config
- Certificates
    - Configuring anonymous authentication in IIS
    - Creating and administering server certificates
- Custom authentication
    - Active Directory users and MCMS subscriber groups
    - Forms-based authentication
- Summary of authentication recommendations
    - Intranet site authentication
    - Extranet site authentication
    - Internet site authentication
    - Web farms

With MCMS, authentication is important because different users may have rights to view, contribute, or administer content using tools and procedures that you wouldn't want just anyone to have access to. To obtain *credentials*—and subsequently authentication—MCMS users must have either a Windows 2000 account or an Active Directory service account.

A variety of authentication options are available. The method best suited for your installation depends on security, simplicity, and other requirements.

Windows Accounts

MCMS works with all Windows 2000 authentication modes. For most MCMS installations, Microsoft recommends Integrated Windows authentication, which uses user data from the client computer for authentication. Credentials are hashed—processed one-way only—which is very difficult to decrypt. This mode takes advantage of existing Windows NT or Active Directory accounts. This is a good option if the MCMS site is secured behind a firewall, if you need a familiar solution, if there are no "public" areas for which users need no authentication, or if Internet Explorer is the sole browser supported. Integrated Windows authentication is best suited for a domain with both user and Web server computer accounts and is compatible with both NTLM and Kerberos transaction security.

■**Note** Kerberos is an encrypted network authentication protocol (RFC 1510) that uses a key distribution service. Authentication is secure because it does not transact user names and passwords in plaintext, does not rely on the host operating system, does not base trust on IP addresses, and does not require physical security on the host. The client and server are mutually authenticated, which prevents spoofing and hijacking. Kerberos can encrypt network traffic. For more information about Kerberos authentication on Windows, refer to the Knowledge Base article, "How to Validate User Credentials on Microsoft Operating Systems" at `http://support.microsoft.com/default.aspx?scid=kb;EN-US;180548`.

■**Note** The NTLM protocol authenticates users and computers based on challenge/response. Under the NTLM protocol, a resource server must contact a domain authentication service on a domain controller for either the computer or user's account. In the absence of a domain, the NTLM protocol can also be used for peer-to-peer authentication. For more information, refer to the XP resource Kit at `http://www.microsoft.com/resources/documentation/Windows/XP/all/reskit/en-us/Default.asp?url=/resources/documentation/Windows/XP/all/reskit/en-us/prdp_log_hghx.asp`.

You configure Integrated Windows authentication via the Internet Service Manager from IIS.

Task 4-1. Configuring Integrated Windows Authentication

1. Launch the Internet Services Manager (Administrative Tools).

2. Expand the domain node for MCMS, and click Default Web Site.

3. Browse to your MCMS Web application, right-click, and select Properties.

4. Edit anonymous access and authentication control on the Directory Security tab.

5. Select Integrated Windows authentication only in the Authentication Methods dialog box. Click OK to accept the changes.

If you are creating a custom Web Service wrapper for your MCMS site, you may choose to handle authentication via a custom ASP.NET page. If this is the case, you enable Integrated Windows authentication via tags in the Web.config file.

Note Before you proceed with modifying the Web.config file, you should have enabled an MCMS project in Visual Studio .NET and have a previously created Web.config file.

Task 4-2. Modifying Web.config

1. Open your Visual Studio .NET project, browse to the Web application, and open Web.config for editing.

2. Replace the existing <authentication> tag in the Web.config file with the following code:

```
<authentication mode="Windows" />
```

3. Replace the existing <authorization> tag in the Web.config file with the following code:

```
<authorization>
<deny users="?" />
</authorization>
```

4. Save changes.

5. Rebuild the Web Service by selecting Build Solution.

After the Web.config file is modified, use the SCA to configure authentication options, such as disabling guest access.

Forms-Based Authentication Using IIS

Forms-based authentication uses ASP.NET pages to acquire user input and perform authentication. After credentials are verified, a cookie containing a *ticket* is issued. From then on, the cookie is polled to verify authentication.

Forms-based authentication should be conducted over Secure Sockets Layer (SSL) to prevent a cookie attack. This MCMS SSL connection provides mutual authentication (clients and servers authenticate one another) and encrypted communication. Malicious users will not be able to use passwords or data they try to intercept.

■**Caution** Forms-based authentication may degrade performance under high traffic volume.

Forms-based authentication solves a few potential problems:

- Supporting browsers (and operating systems) other than Windows Internet Explorer 6.0 and above

- Providing your own form as the logon page user interface (UI)

- Storing private user name/password

- Deploying your MCMS site outside a firewall

- Configuring public (available to anonymous users) and private (available only to users with credentials) pages on your site

Forms-based authentication should not be considered lightly because it is the most complex of the basic authentication schemes. To implement forms-based authentication, you may need to configure IIS to support anonymous login, enable SSL, create a suitable login page, and configure Web.config.

Anonymous User Access

Anonymous user access (Guest account) permits users to access at least some of the (MCMS) Web site without credentials. You can add the guest account to the subscriber rights group using Site Manager. Enabling anonymous access ensures that no conflict occurs between the forms-based authentication scheme and any security that has been previously established in Windows.

Task 4-3. Configuring Anonymous Login Using the IIS Service Manager

1. Launch Internet Services Manager (Administrative Tools), expand the IIS domain node, and open the Default Web Site.

2. Browse to your MCMS Web application, and then view the Properties on the virtual directory where the MCMS applications are stored.

3. Edit Anonymous Access and Authentication on the Directory Security tab.

4. Select only Anonymous Access for Editing in the Authentication Methods dialog box— no other Windows check boxes should be checked.

5. Browse the Anonymous User Account dialog box and select the target computer in the Select User dialog box.

6. Select user `IUSR_<computername>` (Name/In Folder). Select Allow IIS to Control Password in the Anonymous User Account dialog box and then save and verify your changes.

Secure Sockets Layer (SSL)

SSL supports HTTP (or secure HTTPS) by securing transmissions in the following ways:

- Encrypting data
- Providing a secure connection (mutually secured between source and destination)

SSL implementation requires the acquisition of a digital certificate for your authentication server.

Task 4-4. Acquiring a Digital Certificate

1. Launch the Internet Services Manager (Administrative Tools), expand your application's domain node, and select Default Web Site.

2. Browse to your MCMS Web application and view Properties.

3. Select Server Certificate in the Secure Communications section of the Default Web Site dialog box on the Directory Security tab.

4. Assign an existing certificate or import a certificate from a backup file in the Welcome to the Web Server Certificate Wizard.

5. Complete the IIS Web Server Certificate Wizard.

Logon Page

You'll need to create (design and code) a logon page for either or both the MCMS Web Author and (Office) Authoring Connector.

Note You'll find a prototype logon page (ManualLogin.aspx) in the WoodgroveNet sample site (<InstallDrive>:/Program Files/Microsoft Content Manage➡ ment Server/Sample data/WoodgroveNet/Templates).

Task 4-5. Creating a Logon Page

1. Launch Visual Studio .NET, open your MCMS Web Application Project, and browse to your Web application.

2. Select your Web application in Solution Explorer and click Add New Item.

3. In the Categories pane, select Web Project Items from the Add New Item window, and then select Web Form (Templates pane).

4. Name your login page (MyLogonPage.aspx) and open the page for editing.

   The Web.config <authentication> tag uses the name MyLogonPage.aspx to find the logon page.

5. Scroll down to the pageLayout property in the Properties window, and change the layout from GridLayout to FlowLayout.

Task 4-6. Laying Out a Logon Page

The login page (MyLogonPage.aspx) needs controls to provide user access (labels and buttons), and handlers to process event (clicks and key presses). Labels should at least include

Name: (MyDomain/MyUsername)
Password:

1. Drag and drop a Label control and give it a caption such as "Enter username and password."

2. Drag and drop a Name (MyDomain/MyUsername) text control onto the logon page.

3. Drag and drop a Password control next to the Password label.

4. Drag and drop Reset and Submit buttons onto the logon page.

5. For each control dropped onto the page, select Run As Server Control.

Task 4-7. Adding Event Handlers

1. Add an event handler to process a Submit button, and then click `Submit1_ServerClick` for the `MyLogonPage.aspx` logon page:

```
CmsAuthenticationTicket ticket;
ticket = CmsFormsAuthentication.AuthenticateAsUser(
    strServerAccount,
    strServerPassword,
    txtUserName.Text,
    "FirstName");
if( ticket != null )
{
    string strReturnUrl = Request.QueryString["ReturnUrl"];
    CmsFormsAuthentication.SetAuthCookie(ticket, true, false);
    StringBuilder strUrl = new StringBuilder();
    strUrl.Append("http://");
    strUrl.Append(Environment.MachineName);
    strUrl.Append(strReturnUrl);
    Response.Redirect(strUrl.ToString());
}
else
{
    Label1.Text = "Your username or password is incorrect.";
}
49. Add the following code to the Page_Load handler:
if(!Request.IsSecureConnection)
{
    StringBuilder strSSL = new StringBuilder();
    strSSL.Append("https://");
    strSSL.Append(Environment.MachineName);
    strSSL.Append("/");
    strSSL.Append(Request.Url.PathAndQuery);
    Response.Redirect(strSSL.ToString());
}
```

2. Save your changes.

3. Build the Web application by selecting Build Solution.

At this point, a logon page has been implemented. Next, the `Web.config` file must be configured to poll for authentication.

Web.config

Authenticating content contributors is a key element of administering an MCMS installation. Tags in the Web.config file specific to MCMS Web Author and Authoring Connector provide forms-based authentication.

Two similar procedures follow: one to configure forms-based authentication for Authoring Connector and the other to configure forms-based authentication for your MCMS Web site. Make sure you create a separate Web.config file in a separate folder for Authoring Connector. Web.config is located in the Program Files/Microsoft Content Management Server/Server/MCMS folder.

Task 4-8. Configuring Web.config for Authoring Connector

1. Launch Windows Explorer and navigate to Program Files/Microsoft Content ➡ Management Server/Server/MCMS/.

2. Copy Web.config. Navigate to <InstallDrive>:/Program Files/Microsoft ➡ Content Management Server/Server and create a new folder named ACWebApplication.

3. Paste the new copy of Web.config into the ACWebApplication folder.

4. Launch Internet Services Manager (Administrative Tools).

5. Launch the Virtual Directory Wizard by right-clicking the Default Web Site node.

6. On the Virtual Directory Alias page, type **ACWebApplication** in the Alias box, and continue the wizard.

7. On the Web Site Content Directory page, browse to select your new folder (Program Files/Microsoft Content Management Server/Server/ACWebApplication) and continue the wizard.

8. Set Access Permissions to Read, Run Scripts, Execute. Finish the wizard.

9. Select ACWebApplication in the IIS window. Right-click to create a new Virtual Directory and launch the Virtual Directory Creation Wizard.

10. Add MCMS as an alias in the Alias box on the Virtual Directory Alias page, and continue.

11. On the Web Site Content Directory page, browse to select Program Files/Micro➡ soft Content Management Server/Server/IIS_CMS; continue the wizard.

12. Set Access Permissions to Read, Run Scripts, Execute. Finish the wizard.

Use the following procedure for forms-based authentication.

Task 4-9. Configuring `Web.config` for Forms-Based Authentication

1. Launch Visual Studio .NET.

2. Open the solution file for your Web application or Authoring Connector Web application.

3. Open `Web.config` for editing in the Solution Explorer window.

4. Use the following code to replace the existing `<authentication>` tag:

```
<authentication mode="Forms">
    <forms name="MyCookie" path="/" logonUrl="MyLogonPage.aspx"
      protection="All" timeout="30">
    </forms>
</authentication>
```

5. Use the following code to replace the `<authentication>` tag to configure an Authoring Connector logon page:

```
<authentication mode="Forms">
<forms name="MyCookie" path="/"
  loginUrl="/WoodgroveNet/Templates/ManualLogon.aspx"
protection="All"  timeout="30" >
...</forms>
</authentication>
```

6. Use the following code to replace the existing `<authorization>` tag:

```
<authorization>
    <allow users="*" />
</authorization>
```

7. Save your changes by selecting Save All.

8. Rebuild your Web application by selecting Build Solution.

■**Note** Authentication will cascade to an automatic logon page if `Web.config` is set up to deny anonymous users. Ultimately, if the unauthenticated user does not have rights to view that page (in either permission set), the user may enter an infinite authentication loop with `AutoLogon.aspx`.

After Web.config is modified to support authentication, cookie parameters may be modified to automate access to the Web site. Guest access may also be enabled for a public area.

Certificates

With a certificate for authentication, a logon page is not required. When the computer tries to access a server, a digital "key" (installed on the client computer) is automatically authenticated by either a Windows domain account or an Active Directory directory service account. From the perspective of the client, security is seamless and automated. Certificate authentication is effective for a variety of reasons:

- It's a very secure solution, including mutual authentication.
- Forms-based authentication may not be a viable solution, either because you want simple client access or there is automated business-to-business transaction processing.
- You want to partition off other servers that may be accessible via Windows accounts.
- You don't want to manage authentication (a third party negotiates the relationship between the server and the client's certificate).

Configuring Anonymous Authentication in IIS

One important wrinkle you may want to add to certificate authentication is allowing users without certificates to log in as guests so they can view a "public" share. Users with certificates have permissions to view more and/or perform operations such as contributing content. We'll begin by configuring anonymous authentication in IIS.

Task 4-10. Configuring Anonymous Access

1. Launch the Internet Services Manager (Administrative Tools), expand the domain node in which your MCMS application is stored, and select Default Web Site.

2. Browse to your MCMS Web application, select the MCMS virtual directory, and view Properties.

3. Edit the Anonymous Access and Authentication control in the Properties dialog box on the Directory Security tab.

4. Select Anonymous Access and clear any other Windows check boxes.

5. Edit the Authentication Methods dialog box.

6. Browse to select the User dialog box from the Anonymous User Account dialog box.

7. Select `IUSR_<computername>` (Name/In Folder box).

8. Select Allow IIS to Control Password in the Anonymous User Account dialog box.

9. Save your changes and exit the Internet Services Manager.

IIS anonymous access is now configured. Next, you'll create certificate mappings.

Creating and Administering Server Certificates

You can map certificates to domain or Active Directory accounts. If you need to authenticate individual users, you can use a technique known as one-to-one mapping, in which a certificate is mapped to an individual account. There is no limit on one-to-one mapping if you use Active Directory mapping.

If you need to authenticate all the users from a particular group or organization, you can use many-to-one mapping, in which, for example, any certificate containing a common company name is mapped to a single account.

Use the following procedure to create and administer server certificates.

Task 4-11. Administering Server Certificates

1. Launch the Internet Services Manager (Administrative Tools), expand the domain node in which your MCMS application is located, and select Default Web Site.

2. Browse to your MCMS Web application, and select Server Certificate from Secure Communications on the Directory Security tab of the Default Web Site dialog box.

3. Create a certificate using the Certificate Wizard, assign an existing certificate or import a certificate from a backup file, and then finish the IIS Web Server Certificate Wizard.

4. Deploy the client certificate to the client workstation.

■**Note** For additional information about deploying certificates, refer to "Certificates How To" at `http://www.microsoft.com/technet/prodtechnol/windowsserver2003/library/ServerHelp/fb037b9f-8956-411c-a3e8-ce1dfe37da11.mspx`. For additional information about mapping rules, refer to `http://go.microsoft.com/fwlink/?LinkId=9689`.

> ■**Note** Certificate authentication is an expensive proposition. The cost of issuing and managing client certificates may easily overshadow its value.

You have finished certificate authentication. Next, you can configure settings in the SCA.

Custom Authentication

Custom authentication works well for sites with a minimal number of types of subscribers—the example Microsoft uses is employee, partner, and public access. Explore custom authentication as an option if

- The primary use of your site is by anonymous users
- Access to content is subjugated to MCMS roles
- You want to use an external authentication source—as is the case with a profiler
- You use an internal site for authoring (and deploy to a production site)

> ■**Caution** One-to-one or many-to-one mappings of external users to Active Directory users is better suited to certificate authentication, as covered in the previous section.

From the UI perspective, custom authentication and forms-based authentication are similar. If a user attempts access to a privileged page or folder—or attempts to perform a procedure such as submitting content—a custom page is displayed that processes the request by identifying the Active Directory account mapping required. If successful, the user may be logged on as the mapped user.

> ■**Note** Typically, custom authentication is processed by mapping external users to Active Directory accounts; however, MCMS users may be authenticated against a source other than Active Directory directory service.

Active Directory Users and MCMS Subscriber Groups

To begin, you need to create a specific user account for each type of user access you want to grant. To do this, you'll repeat the following procedure for each type of user access. After this is complete, you'll map the users to MCMS subscriber groups, for which the appropriate rights have been granted.

Task 4-12. Creating MCMS Accounts

1. On the domain controller, launch the Computer Management tool (Administrative Tools).

2. Expand Local Users and Groups, and select New User. Create the user to represent the type of access you want.

3. Repeat for each type of access.

After creating the MCMS accounts, create MCMS subscriber groups using Site Manager to differentiate each type of access. Map the Active Directory users to their corresponding subscriber group.

Note No duplicate MCMS rights group names are allowed.

Task 4-13. Creating Rights Groups

1. Launch the MCMS Site Manager, and then log on as an administrator.

2. Select User Roles and use the context menu to choose New Rights Group.

3. Enter a name for the rights group by clicking Rename.

4. View the Properties of your new rights group.

5. Enter a description for the rights group (max 256 characters).

After you have created the rights group, you need to complete the process by adding your user accounts as members.

Task 4-14. Adding Members to Rights Groups

1. Launch Site Manager and log on as an administrator.

2. Select User Roles and the user role to which you want to add a user.

3. View the Properties for the target rights group and your user on the Modify the Group Members tab.

4. Select a domain.

5. Add groups or individual users.

6. Save your changes and exit the Site Manager.

Finally, you must assign containers to your rights group, so the users in that rights group are subscribed to the container. After you are working in your production site, you can view Properties on a container, and check the Rights tab to display a list of assignees.

Caution You're live! Any changes you make to the Group Rights tab take effect immediately. (Notice the disabled Cancel button.) To undo, you must manually reassign containers.

Task 4-15. Assigning Containers to Rights Groups

1. Launch Site Manager and log on as an administrator.

2. Select User Roles and the rights group for which you will assign containers.

3. View the Properties by selecting the Group Rights tab of the <rights group name> Properties dialog box. Container hierarchies are displayed.

4. Assign containers in one of two ways:

   • To assign one container, click the container name; the X changes to a check mark.

   • To assign a container and all its subcontainers, select Propagate Rights to Children from the context menu. All Xs change to check marks.

5. Save your changes.

The process is complete. You have enabled users to work specific MCMS workspaces with appropriate permissions to containers.

Forms-Based Authentication

Microsoft provides example code to put in your logon page to perform the following actions:

- Acquire an (external) user's credentials
- Verify the credentials against a third-party source
- Map the user to an Active Directory user
- Authenticate the user to MCMS using AuthenticateAsUser

Task 4-16. Creating Custom Logon Pages

1. Add the following Microsoft sample code to your logon page:

```
private bool AuthenticateMappedClientAccount
( string clientAccountName,
               string clientAccountType )
{
    string serverAccountName;
    string serverAccountPassword;
    // map the client to an Active Directory user
    // to do: create the function MappedServerAccount
    serverAccountName = MappedServerAccount(
            clientAccountName, clientAccountType )
    // retrieve Active Directory password
    // to do: create the function RetrieveAccountPassword
    serverAccountPassword =
            RetrieveAccountPassword( serverAccountName );
    CmsAuthenticationTicket ticket =
        CmsFormsAuthentication.AuthenticateAsUser(
            serverAccountName,
            serverAccountPassword,
            clientAccountName,
            clientAccountType );
    if ( ticket != null )
    {
        // parameters: CmsAuthenticationTicket, setAspNetCookie,
           createPersistentCookie
        CmsFormsAuthentication.
         RedirectFromLoginPage( ticket, true, false );
        return true;
    }
```

```
    else
    {
        return false;
    }
}
```

2. Test the function to verify that it maps an external user to an Active Directory user and authenticates the mapped Active Directory user to MCMS.

You have configured custom authentication. You can now configure settings in the SCA.

Summary of Authentication Recommendations

Microsoft recommends one of three MCMS authentication scenarios:

- To support intranet sites
- To support extranet sites
- To support Internet sites

Intranet Site Authentication

From the standpoint of security, an internal, corporate intranet site, which doesn't allow anonymous access, requires the simplest authentication. "Simple" may belie the effort required to set up and administer MCMS; however, corporate intranets typically have some security in place:

- Integrated Windows authentication
- Firewall protection
- Only Internet Explorer as the Internet browser
- Configured for internal user authoring only

MCMS access on an intranet site is configured using IIS for Web configuration, Web.config to configure ASP.NET, and the SCA to set MCMS parameters.

Extranet Site Authentication

MCMS extranet sites use forms-based authentication. Often extranet sites allow guest access with no login, although content contributors or administrative personnel are required to have an Active Directory directory service account for logging on and must provide a password or a certificate. Security is more complex on extranet sites because

- You may need to support multiple browser technologies.

- No firewall security may be in place.

- Authoring may be done by external users; pages may be located on the production site.

- Authentication may be handled by applications outside the Active Directory account system, for example, Microsoft Passport or Microsoft Commerce Server.

- Content may be protected by MCMS rights groups.

Microsoft recommends authenticating external sites using either forms-based authentication, certificates, or custom authentication.

Internet Site Authentication

A public site with guest-only authentication requires no logon unless you are using a profiling system. After IIS is configured to allow anonymous login, it requires no other modification. Web.config, however, is used to configure the ASP.NET forms-based authentication so you'll need to remove the MCMS authorization module:

```
<add type=
"Microsoft.ContentManagement.Web.Security.CmsAuthorizationModule,
Microsoft.ContentManagement.Web, Version=5.0.1200.0, Culture=neutral,
PublicKeyToken=31bf3856ad364e35" name="CmsAuthorizationModule" />
```

You also need to specify an existing domain account for use as the guest account. Remember to add this account to a subscribers rights group.

Web Farms

Web farms require synchronization of server keys and sharing encryption key values. MCMS uses server keys for encryption when creating authentication tickets for browsing. The server keys must be identical across a cluster to use cookies for authentication. Without synchronization, reauthentication is likely every time the user browses a new server.

Use Managekey to export server encryption keys across the cluster. You must run the Managekey.exe file on each server in the cluster, and use Import Key to synchronize key settings.

▪Note Server key data is extremely sensitive. For additional information about best security practices, refer to `http://go.microsoft.com/fwlink/?LinkId=9531`.

ASP.NET encrypts (hashes) data so it is only accessible from the server that created the data. In a Web farm, each server needs to share the same machine key. Machine Key setting encrypts or decrypts data, as shown in Table 4-1.

Table 4-1. *Machine Key Settings*

Attribute	Description
ValidationKey	The ValidationKey attribute validates authentication cookies; Autogenerate is the default, but it can be manually configured.
Validation	The Validation attribute determines what hashing scheme is computed. Valid values include MD5, SHA1, or 3DES. The hash can be sent to the client and the server can validate the data in the cookie by rehashing the values with the ValidationKey attribute. If the values match, the data are considered valid.
DecryptionKey	The DecryptionKey attribute is used to encrypt authentication cookie data. The ASP.NET default is autogenerated, but for server clusters, you must set a custom value. Each server in the Web farm needs to use an identical value.

▪Note For additional information about ASP.NET `machine.config`, refer to `http://go.microsoft.com/fwlink/?LinkId=9599`.

Be careful when creating user accounts that operate over Web farm clusters. Local users and groups apply across all computers in the cluster. This can create unintentional access issues. This also means that you can configure a guest user across a cluster without a domain controller by setting the guest user and creating the account on all servers in the cluster.

Summary

This chapter covered Windows account security, including forms-based authentication, anonymous user access, and secure sockets. We provided a simplistic logon template and showed how to configure `Web.config` to use it.

This chapter also covered certificates and custom authentication scenarios, and provided a brief summary of authentication recommendations.

PART 2

Administration and Deployment

■ ■ ■

CHAPTER 5

Administration and Support

This chapter covers

- Server administration using SCA
  - Setting the site content entry point
  - ASP compatibility
  - URLs
  - Channel-to-host mapping
  - Full-text search and indexing
  - MCMS security issues
- Supporting authors, editors, and approvers
  - Authoring content
  - Managing the publication of content

In addition to initial installation and configuration, the MCMS requires periodic adjustment and operational support. Some tasks, when performed, take effect locally and some globally, such as changes to a database. In this chapter, we'll cover making changes to an MCMS. Tools are provided by the MCMS environment to manage local server properties. At the end of the chapter, we'll describe an important, and potentially time-consuming, task: supporting content authors.

Server Administration Using SCA

Administrators (requires administrator rights) use the MCMS Server Configuration Application (SCA) for configuration and general maintenance.

■**Note** Refer to Chapter 2 for details of how to configure the SCA initially. A port number of 80 is the default, assumed port. If the SCA's port has another number, include the port number in the URL.

Remote administration using the SCA requires SSL to be configured on both the client and the server computer.

The SCA can be made available over a secure port using SSL for remote access. To implement SSL, install a digital certificate on the server.

You acquire server certificates from an outside certification authority or issue your own using Microsoft Certificate Services. The process of acquiring certificates from a certification authority is outside the scope of this chapter; however, Microsoft recommends some questions you should ask when choosing an authority:

- What are the initial costs, renewal costs, and other service costs?
- Will the certificate be compatible with all supported browsers?
- Will the certificate system serve IIS Web Server Certificate Wizard requests?
- How secure is my installation? Is the authority trusted?

Microsoft recommends some guidelines when opting for issuing your own server certificates. Note that Microsoft Certificate Services supports multiple certificate formats, auditing, and logging; however, integrating Certificate Services with existing security systems takes an investment in time.

Following are Microsoft guidelines when assigning IP addresses, Web sites, and SSL ports to certificates:

- Cannot assign multiple server certificates per site
- Can assign one certificate to multiple sites
- Can assign multiple IP addresses per site
- Can assign multiple SSL ports per site

Use either the Web Server Certificate Wizard or Certificate Manager (MMC "Certificates") to export and back up your server certificates.

By configuring a certificate trust list (CTL), you manage which client certificates are to be accepted. CTLs are not available for FTP sites.

Task 5-1. Creating a CTL

1. Launch IIS Manager.

2. Expand the local computer and the Web Sites folder.

3. Select a Web site and view Properties.

4. Click Edit on the Directory Security tab, under Secure Communications.

5. To enable a CTL, select the Enable Certificate Trust List check box.

6. To create a new CTL, click New; to edit an existing CTL, click Edit.

7. Finish the Certificate Trust List Wizard.

Use IIS Service Manager to enable certificates.

Task 5-2. Enabling Server Certificates

1. Launch Internet Services Manager (Administrative Tools).

2. Expand the domain node, and select the Default Web Site.

3. Browse to the MCMS Web application and view Properties.

4. In Secure Communications on the Directory Security tab, select Server Certificate.

5. Use the Welcome to the Web Server Certificate Wizard to assign or import a certificate.

6. Finish the IIS Web Server Certificate Wizard.

Task 5-3. Launching SCA

You may launch the SCA from the browser or by using Start ➤ Programs. To access the browser:

1. Enter the SCA URL on the browser's address bar (<computername> corresponds to the computer containing the SCA Web site; port # is required *if not set to 80*):

   `http://<computername>:<port #>/NRConfig`

Setting the Content Site Entry Point

Setting the entry point affects only the server on which it is set.

Note ASP-based Web site authoring options are set in the file `<drive:>\`
`Program Files\Microsoft Content Management Server\Server\IIS_NR\`
`System\WBC\Customizable\OptionsServer.inc`.

ASP-based Web site options, for read only, are set in the file `<drive:>\`
`Program Files\Microsoft Content Management Server\Server\`
`IIS_NR_RO_ASP\System\WBC\Customizable\OptionsServer_RT.inc`.

Task 5-4. Setting the Web Entry Point

1. Launch the SCA.

2. Select the Web tab of the MCMS Configuration Application dialog box.

3. In the MCMS column for the specific Web site, select the appropriate value.

4. Close the application.

ASP Compatibility Mode

ASP.NET mode restricts all read-only sites to ASP.NET-based content. Mixed mode supports read-only and read/write sites that use both Active Server Pages (ASP) and ASP.NET-based content. Use the SCA to view ASP compatibility mode. You cannot change the ASP compatibility mode without uninstalling and reinstalling MCMS.

Task 5-5. Viewing ASP Compatibility Mode

1. Launch the SCA.

2. Select the General tab.

3. ASP compatibility mode is displayed in the Server ASP Compatibility Mode box in the General Configuration dialog box.

URLs

With the SCA, you can specify how MCMS references pages: congruent with channel directory structure (hierarchical, the default method) or by assigning individual (random, unique IDs) names to pages. Channel-based (hierarchy) URLs are easier to use because the URLs are congruent with the MCMS directory structure and provide better Internet search engine compatibility.

Note MCMS names are comprised of Unicode (UTF-8 encoded) characters. Use characters 0 to 9 and A to Z. Some non-Roman characters may not work properly. Some search engines cannot index pages where the URL contains the characters: ()@?#$%^&*. If you directly type a URL in your Web browser's Address box, you must manually replace the invalid character with its URL-encoded equivalent. The .htm file name extension is optional for requested pages.

Task 5-6. Setting the URL Format

1. Launch the SCA.

2. Select Configure on the General tab.

3. From the URL Format drop-down list, select Hierarchical or Unique ID.

4. Save your changes and close the SCA.

Channel-to-Host Mapping

Channel-to-host header name mapping virtualizes domains; that is, it allows users to view content across domains transparently (by using the channel name instead of the entire domain name, concatenated with the computer, concatenated with the channel name). Channel-to-host maps require registration of host header names with DNS (Domain Name System) and, if applicable, WINS (Windows Internet Name Service) servers.

Task 5-7. Mapping Channel Names to Host Header Names

1. Launch the SCA.

2. Select Configure on the General tab.

3. Select Yes from the Map Channel Names to Host Header Names drop-down list.

4. Save changes and close the SCA.

Full-Text Search and Indexing

Web crawlers that provide *full-text search* or those that index a site for an Internet search engine can be purchased from third-party vendors. Web crawlers begin at top-level pages, trace the links, and store the information to guide crawler searches.

■**Note** For additional information about searching an MCMS site, refer to `http://go.microsoft.com/fwlink/?LinkId=8426`. For recommendations on search engine indexing, refer to `http://go.microsoft.com/fwlink/?LinkId=12312`.

Following are W3C recommendations to help make your site more accessible to search engines:

- Define the human language of the page; provide `Link` tags to reference alternate translations (enables search results in the user's language). Add a `Link` tag in the header for each alternative language translation:

  ```
  <LINK rel="alternate" type="text/html" href=[document]
  hreflang="[language]"
  lang=" [language]" title="[title in alternate language]" >
  ```

- Add `META` tags for keywords/phrases (a comma-separated list) or a short description:

  ```
  <META name="keywords" content="[keyword1,keyword2,keyword3,...]">
  <META name="description" content="[descriptive phrase]">
  ```

  A search returns the keywords.

- Reference the home page of a subweb using a `LINK` tag with `rel="start"`:

  ```
  <LINK rel="start" type="text/html
  href="[home page]" title="[title]">
  ```

- Provide a `robots.txt` file to specify pages that *index bots* can access:

  ```
  User-agent: *     # applies to all robots
  Disallow: /       # disallow indexing of all pages
  ```

  One `User-agent` field must be provided for each record. The `Disallow` field specifies a partial URI that is not to be visited.

■**Note** An *Index Bot* checks for `http://www.[domain name].com/robots.txt`, that is, the root directory of the site. There can only be one root directory per site. If it finds `robots.txt`, it checks to see if it is allowed to save (index) page information. `robots.txt` can apply to specific robots. `[URL]/robots.txt` is case-sensitive (must be lowercase). Sample `robots.txt` files are available at:

- `http://www.w3.org/ http://www.w3.org/robots.txt`

- `http://www.w3.org:80/ http://www.w3.org:80/robots.txt`

- `http://www.w3.org:1234/ http://www.w3.org:1234/robots.txt`

- `http://w3.org/ http://w3.org/robots.txt`

- A `META` tag can be employed to enable or disallow Index Bots:

  `<META name="ROBOTS" content="NOINDEX, NOFOLLOW">`

  Options include `ALL`, `INDEX`, `NOFOLLOW`, and `NOINDEX`.

- Search engines generally display the contents of the `<TITLE>` tag for indexed pages. The MCMS Publishing API supports programmatically setting a title based on a template and placeholder data.

Default guest access must be enabled to allow search engines to index a site. Set default guest access using the SCA. To allow full-text search, IIS Basic Authentication must be set.

■**Caution** Use IIS Basic Authentication cautiously because it causes passwords to be sent as plaintext.

Task 5-8. Enabling Basic Authentication

1. Launch IIS Manager.
2. View Properties for the Web server that is hosting the MCMS site.
3. Edit Anonymous Access and Authentication on the Directory Security tab.
4. Select Basic Authentication.
5. Save changes and close the IIS Manager.

Guest access permits users to access some or all of the MCMS Web pages without providing authentication credentials. The system will not grant default guest users any rights greater than those a subscriber has, regardless of what kind of rights group is actually responsible for providing the account with rights. A minimum level of subscriber rights is required before any information about an object is disclosed.

If the guest account is enabled, users are granted the rights they have explicitly been assigned plus all the rights that are assigned to the guest user. Which pages the anonymous user is allowed to access depends on the permissions of the subscriber group or groups to which the administrator assigns the guest account. The guest account must be added to the subscriber rights group using the MCMS Site Manager. For more information, see Task 4-13, "Creating Rights Groups," in Chapter 4.

Task 5-9. Enabling Guest Access

1. Launch the SCA.

2. Select the Security tab of the Security Configuration dialog box.

3. Configure Guest Visitors:

   - Allow Guests On Site (select Yes or No).

   - Type (domain\user name) or browse to find the name of the Guest Login Account.

4. Save changes and close the SCA.

MCMS Security Issues

Three security issues must be addressed: domain accounts, cookies, and object locks.

MCMS System Account and Domains

You can only specify a system account in a supported domain. To specify a system account from a large domain without being able to view all its members, prepend the domain to the name of the account: <domain>\<username>. Alternatively, you may add the entire domain, which may be necessary if users from the domain contribute content or otherwise participate in the publication process.

Task 5-10. Adding a Domain

1. Launch the SCA.

2. Enter or browse to the Windows NT domain to be added. Select Add on the Access tab.

3. Save changes and close the SCA.

To add local accounts (Everyone/Authenticated Users) to a rights group, add the local computer as a domain.

Cookies

MCMS stores encrypted authentication tickets in cookies. Refer to Chapter 4 for more information about MCMS 2002 authentication.

Task 5-11. Setting Cookie Parameters

1. Launch the SCA.

2. Configure the Security Configuration dialog box by using the Security tab.

3. Set Web Browser Cookie Settings:

   - Cookie Lifetime (minutes)

   - Check Machine IP Against Cookie (select Yes or No)

4. Save settings and close the SCA.

Managing Object Locks

An object, such as a page, undergoing editing is locked to prevent multiple users from trying to make changes at the same time. (Users can have read-only access to a locked object.) If a client session was terminated while one or more objects locked, the object(s) remain locked and inaccessible. An administrator must use the Kill Lock command (in the Tools menu of the MCMS Site Manager) to unlock the object before editing can proceed.

It is important to make sure no one is using the object at the time a Kill Lock command is selected or data loss will result.

Supporting Authors, Editors, and Approvers

The value of MCMS lies in its capability to facilitate a group of business information workers who collaborate via portal. They maintain and contribute content specific to their business requirements on their own, without outside IT staff having to convert the information to a Web-enabled form and control its deployment. The efficiency of this model, however, hinges on the amount of support required to enable nontechnical, non-IT staff to function as authors, editors, and approvers—to manage the flow of information to their Web portal.

Authoring Content

Editing and submitting content postings is a familiar process to anyone with Web publishing experience. Not all MCMS content contributors, however, share this skill set. Be sensitive to the needs of these authors. You may want to create a brief training document (or help system) and post instructions such as are presented in the following two authoring procedures.

The MCMS Web Author

The MCMS 2002 Web Author provides two functions: limiting access to data and providing a UI for authors to edit and post content. The Web Author also enables editors and moderators to approve, publish, or decline content submitted by authors. The Web Author, therefore, has two modes:

- **Presentation mode**: In this browse mode, Web Author restricts links to published and approved content.

- **Authoring mode**: Authors, editors, and moderators post new content, edit previously published content, delete existing postings, or approve/decline submitted postings.

The Web Author console provides command controls and status controls. Controls are hidden from the user until entering Authoring mode.

■Note If you are evaluating MCMS, use the WoodgroveNet sample site to test editing procedures.

Explore Presentation mode before editing. Anonymous Access is enabled, so no password is required. Next, log in to the site using an account from the Authors group. Microsoft recommends the following procedure: Navigate to Small Business/Case Studies. Select Blue Yonder Airlines and choose Switch to Edit Site. Examine the Web Author options. Note the restricted rights for the Careers/About Us channel.

Task 5-12. Editing and Submitting Content (Web Author)

1. Launch your Internet browser and navigate to the MCMS write-enabled site. Log on and select a page to edit.

2. After the page loads, enter Authoring mode (the command or link varies from site to site; the default is Switch to Edit Site).

3. The Web Author console appears (the position and configuration varies depending on how the console has been configured; the default is positioned at the top of the page).

4. Scroll to a placeholder (the symbols in the upper-right corner of the placeholder indicates the type of data the placeholder is configured for).

5. Scroll to a text indicating an existing hyperlink or select text to create a hyperlink. Select Edit Hyperlink on the console toolbar. Enter the hyperlink by assigning the typical properties: a URL and an ALT tag for the link. Choose Open Link or New Unnamed Window.

6. Save your edits.
   Information about page status and version is displayed at the top of the Web Author console.

7. Select Submit on the Web Authoring console; note the Page Status change: Waiting➡ forEditorApproval.

8. Select Approved on the Web Authoring console; note the Page Status change: Published.

9. Log off to exit Web Author mode.

If you have enabled editorial and approval processes, page revisions do not "go live" when an author submits them. Someone with editing/approval privileges on the channel must approve the page.

MCMS (Office) Authoring Connector

Office is integrated with MCMS to provide an integrated portal solution. Word is arguably the most familiar business application in use today. It makes sense to leverage Word's familiar UI whenever possible to minimize support issues. Using Word for page authoring does not require knowledge of Web publishing techniques, familiarity with HTML or other markup languages, or third-party authoring applications. The MCMS Authoring Connector simplifies submission of content even further using predefined tasks associated with customized forms, so users don't even need to select specific page templates or navigate to the appropriate content containers.

> **Note** The MCMS Authoring Connector is compatible with Word 2002 and greater. Word 2002 shipped with Office XP. Unless otherwise mentioned, however, assume that this section refers to Office 2003 and Word 2003.
>
> Refer to Chapter 2 for additional information about installing and configuring the MCMS Authoring Connector.

Using Word with MCMS Authoring Connector installed as a plug-in, an author can create and publish content directly, without the Web Author console. Authoring Connector can render a Word document to HTML (for publication by MCMS) or it can use the content placeholders (for text, graphics, or attachments) located on the template to store page data directly in the Content Repository.

After the Authoring Connector has been installed and configured on the client computer, use the following procedure for authoring and submitting content.

Task 5-13. Editing/Submitting Content (Word/Authoring Connector)

1. Create a Word document with a graphic and text in the normal way, and save your document.

2. Select Send to MCMS to launch the Authoring Template Wizard.

3. Enter basic page information.

4. Set Publishing Dates and Times.

5. Submit the page on the Page Submission dialog box.

6. Preview the page using the Preview Page button.

> **Note** If you are an approver, use the Web Author to approve pages after a new page is made available. Select Approve and the page goes "live."

> **Tip** For more information about templates, content types, and submitting through the Authoring Connector, refer to "Customizing Microsoft Content Management Server 2002 Authoring Connector" at http://go.microsoft.com/fwlink/?LinkId=16803.

Managing the Publication of Content

Typically in a production environment, an author is not the only contributor to the publication process. The Web Author console also supports editors, moderators, and approvers. MCMS 2002 makes it easy for editors to view page modifications before they approve the changes.

Task 5-14. Viewing Revisions and Approving Content

1. Launch your Internet browser and navigate to the MCMS write-enabled site. Log on and select a page to edit.

2. After the page loads, select Edit in the Web Author console.

3. Select Revision History.

4. Select the boxes under the Latest Unapproved and Approved Revisions.

5. Select Compare. The edited page uses color-coding to identify changed elements.

6. Select the Source tab to view the page's underlying HTML markup. Notice the changes are also color-coded for identification.

7. Close the Revision History windows.

8. Select the Approve link if you are satisfied with the changes.

9. If you need to approve multiple pages, select the Approval Assistant link.

10. Check the items to approve (sortable list); select Approve to publish pages as a batch operation.

Summary

Server administration tasks affect the local environment as opposed to the global environment, such as changes to the Content Repository database that is shared among all the MCMS servers. The tool provided for local server administration is the MCMS SCA. The SCA can be enabled for remote administration using an SSL connection.

Server administration is comprised of tasks to manage the MCMS Web site, such as entry points for viewing and authoring, handling ASP-based content, and providing URLs to pages in the site. Of primary importance to the server administrator is making the site accessible. Enabling full-text search and Internet search engines are issues that impact accessibility. The other critical accessibility issue is maintaining security and accessibility concurrently.

Administration also involves supporting the site's users, which in the case of MCMS, includes content contributors and users that manage the publication process. You may decide to distribute the information presented in the last part of this chapter as user training.

CHAPTER 6

■ ■ ■

Administering a Publication Environment

This chapter covers

- The Site Manager
- Rights groups
- Channels
    - Creating channels
    - Managing channels
    - Managing pages
- Resource galleries
    - Managing resource galleries
    - Managing resources
- Templates
    - Managing templates with galleries
    - Managing templates

If you were to read only one chapter, this should be it. The topical coverage of this chapter includes managing container hierarchies and granting access to them based on roles. Evolving a publication environment that facilitates acquiring and presenting content in a cogent way that addresses a business scenario, however, is a much more complex task. Just as we do not discuss business intelligence in this book, we also do not delve into communications topics that might help you organize your business information more logically. As an administrator, however, your job is to guide and assist the portal collaborators so they evolve a business tool that is effective at achieving its goals and efficient in its operation. It's not about the technology, but if the technology is ignored, it's a mess. Okay, now we'll put away the soapbox and get back to the short declarative sentences that outline procedures.

The MCMS publishing environment consists of containers that are used to organize and store pages, resources, and templates, and make them available to authors. Think of it as creating a virtual workspace so that authors and publishers can work efficiently. Data acquisition is facilitated by templates or forms, which MCMS manages. Authors don't have to create Web pages with markup code; they just fill in the blanks on templates. When subscribers make requests, pages are rendered by dynamically inserting data back into templates. Remember, one of the primary objectives of MCMS is to abstract the process of Web publication to a level completely removed from markup language. Templates aid greatly in this process.

Three roles emerge as critical to the process: administrators, channel managers, and template designers. Members of these groups are responsible for creating and maintaining the containers: Channels contain pages, Resource Galleries contain media, and Template Galleries contain page templates. The administrator associates user roles with specific containers. The organizational logic of a site container should be considered carefully to optimize workflow and match user skill sets with appropriate jobs.

MCMS provides the Site Manager application to manage containers.

The Site Manager

The Site Manager client application is used for maintaining container hierarchies. In this chapter, when we refer to logging on to the Site Manager with administrative credentials, we mean either as an administrator, a channel manager, or a template designer.

Task 6-1. Setting Site Manager Options

1. Launch the Site Manager, log on using administrative credentials, and select Start.

2. Select Tools ➤ Options, and then the following:

   • Select Show Warning Before Sending to Deleted Items Bin to Verify Delete.

   • Select Enable Limited or Expanded Export Notice.

   • Select Enable Preview Export Prompt for Confirmation During Export.

3. Save changes.

MCMS stores and retrieves items in the cache whenever the Site Manager makes requests. With concurrent users, the cached version of the container hierarchy needs to be synchronized with the database. Refresh the Site Manager to see the reflected changes.

Task 6-2. Refreshing the Site Manager

To refresh a single item, right-click the item and choose Refresh from the context menu.

To refresh all containers in the Site Manager, use the Global Refresh tool.

Rights Groups

Rights provide users access to specific containers or, in some cases, entire channels. To obtain rights to use items in a container, a user must become a member of an MCMS rights group assigned to the container. Each rights group has permissions associated with one of eight MCMS roles:

- **Subscriber**: Views public channel contents; views private content by permission.

- **Author**: Creates and submits pages; deletes own pages; assigned content permissions per container.

- **Editor**: Author permission, plus approves/declines submitted pages; assigned content permissions per container.

- **Moderator**: Editor permission; assigned content permissions per channel.

- **Resource Manager**: Creates shared resources and galleries; replaces and deletes shared resources in galleries; assigned content permissions per container.

- **Template Designer**: Editor permission; creates resource galleries and template galleries; creates, edits, checks in, and deletes templates; assigns rights groups to containers they own; assigned content permissions per container.

- **Channel Manager**: Full administrator and publishing rights; assigned content permissions per channel.

- **Site Manager**: Full administrator and publishing rights to the entire site.

Note A user with any rights to a container will also have subscription rights, which allows the user to view items in that container.

Administrators have all rights in all containers and administrator rights cannot be removed. Only a few users traditionally hold administrator rights. Channel managers have administrator rights, but only to specific containers.

Note Administrator and channel manager user accounts should be on the same domain as the MCMS.

In this section, we'll cover creating a new rights group, adding members, and assigning the group rights to a container.

Task 6-3. Creating a Rights Group

1. Launch the Site Manager, log on using administrative credentials, and select Start.

2. Select User Roles in the Site Manager window.

3. Right-click the role for which your new group has permission, and then choose New Rights Group. A new rights group is created.

4. Right-click the new rights group and select Rename. Enter a name for the rights group. ·

5. Select the new rights group, and view Properties.

6. Enter a description (256 characters maximum).

7. Save changes.

Note MCMS does not allow duplicate rights group names.

After a rights group is created, members need to be added.

Task 6-4. Adding Members

1. Launch the Site Manager, log on using administrative credentials, and select Start.

2. Select User Roles in the Site Manager window.

3. Right-click on the rights group to which you want to add members and select Properties.

4. Select the Group Members tab in the Properties dialog box, and then choose Modify.

5. From the drop-down box in the upper-right corner, select Select from List of All Groups and Users.

6. Select a domain. If new users were recently created, select Synchronize to update the list of users (can take 10 minutes to fully synchronize).

7. Move Groups or Users to the Rights Groups Members section.

8. Exit the Site Manager.

■**Note** You cannot view users from a nontrusted domain. To work around this, create an identical (names and passwords) account in both domains.

After a rights group has been created and members added, select containers in which members can work. Subscription rights to a container are automatically set when a rights group is assigned to any container.

■**Note** After a container has been assigned to a rights group, the users in that rights group are automatically subscribed to that container.

■**Tip** Add Windows 2000 security groups to rights group, rather than adding members individually. Rights groups will update automatically.

Make sure subscribers have view rights to parent containers. If they don't, they cannot view items in the child containers, even if they have rights to the child container.

Task 6-5. Assigning a Rights Group to a Container

1. Launch the Site Manager, log on using administrative credentials, and select Start.

2. Select User Roles in the Site Manager window.

3. Right-click on the rights group to which you want to add members and select Properties.

4. Select the Group Members tab in the Properties dialog box and then choose Modify.

5. In the Properties dialog box, select the Group Rights tab to display the container hierarchy to which the rights group can be assigned. To get information about a particular container, select the container and view Properties.

6. Assign at least one container from each category:

- To assign a single container, select it (the X changes to a check mark).

- To unassign a single container, select it again (the check mark changes back to an X).

- To assign a container and all its child containers, right-click it and choose Propagate Rights to Children from the context menu.

7. Changes take effect immediately (Cancel is disabled). To undo changes, you must manually reassign containers.

8. Exit the Site Manager.

■Note MCMS provides limited support for Active Directory nested groups on domains. A user can log on to MCMS as members of a subgroup if its parent group is granted rights. You would not be able to administer rights to individual accounts within specific subgroups.

■Note Deleted user names remain in the MCMS database, but the users are no longer able to log on to MCMS.

Channels

MCMS uses channels to store, organize, and manage access to content. MCMS administrators, channel managers, and template designers use Site Manager to create channels for organizing pages.

Channels are the output stream. Templates are saved as *postings*, that is, pages that have linked placeholder text and resources. When the MCMS site goes live, these pages are served to subscribers. In many venues, the templates that are used in the data acquisition are also the templates used in channels (such as with an ISP or technical publication site). In other cases, the content acquired via template in the authoring phase is repurposed and used within other templates for an entirely different look and feel. This might be more the case in an educational site where the same labs and student materials may be modularized and used within many courses.

Creating Channels

Before you set up the channel hierarchy and organize the workspace, you should be aware of MCMS naming conventions:

- Each channel must have a unique name.

- URLs (names of channels and resources) can only contain US-ASCII characters and templates can only contain alphanumeric characters, spaces, and the following symbols: -, _, (,), .

- Do not use #, &, %, +, /, or | characters in a channel name.

- MCMS reserves the characters NR (root virtual directory). Do not name a channel NR.

- Do not use spaces in channel names (spaces are converted to the plus sign [+]).

- Channel names must be fewer than 100 characters in length.

- Do not save a page with the .htm extension (MCMS automatically adds the .htm extension).

Task 6-6. Naming/Describing Channels

1. Launch Site Manager, and log on as channel manager.

2. Select the Channel icon to display channel hierarchy.

3. Use the channel hierarchy to locate where the channel is to be created.

4. Select the location for new channel, right-click, and select New Channel.

5. Set the following options in the New Channel dialog box:

   - Name (component of URL for this new channel and its subchannels)

   - Display Name (meaningful title for the new channel)

   - Description (maximum 255 characters)

   - Use Name (use channel name as Display Name)

After naming and describing the new channel, assign rights to it. When you assign rights groups to a channel, you give users permission to access that channel via a browser.

Note A newly created channel inherits the parent channel's rights groups.

Task 6-7. Assigning Rights Groups to Channels

1. Launch Site Manager and log on as channel manager.

2. Select the Channel icon to display the channel hierarchy.

3. Right-click your new channel and select Properties.

4. On the Rights tab, select Modify.

5. Next to Look in, select the user role from the drop-down list in the Select User Rights for Your New Channel dialog box.

6. Select the desired rights group and choose Add. Alternatively, select Add Parent's Rights to assign the same rights groups as parent.

7. Select OK to save changes.

8. Exit Site Manager.

Managing Channels

You edit certain channel properties by setting them in the Site Manager. These properties include Important Channel, Hide When Published, Web Robots Can Crawl Links, and Web Robots Can Index This Channel's Navigation.

Task 6-8. Modifying Channel Options

1. Launch Site Manager and log on as channel manager.

2. Select the Channel icon to display the channel hierarchy.

3. Right-click your new channel and select Properties.

4. Select the Publishing tab.

5. Set options as desired on the Publishing tab:

   • Important Channel (mark channel as important)

   • Hide When Published (hide content when published)

   • Web Robots Can Crawl Links (allow full-text searches using Internet search engines)

   • Web Robots Can Index This Channel's Navigation (allow content to be indexed by Internet search engines)

6. Select OK to save changes.

7. Exit Site Manager.

You edit the publishing schedule by changing Start and Stop publishing dates.

Task 6-9. Modifying the Publication Schedule

1. Launch Site Manager and log on as channel manager.

2. Select the Channel icon to display the channel hierarchy.

3. Right-click the channel to edit and select Properties.

4. Select the Publishing tab.

5. In the Lifetime section, select Set.

6. Set options in the Start Publishing section:

   • Immediately (allow subscriber to view content immediately)

   • On Select (specify date and time that publishing begins)

7. Set options in the Stop Publishing section:

   • Never Stop Publishing (allow subscribers to view content permanently)

   • Interval (specify time after which channel will expire relative to the Start Publishing date)

   • On (specify date and time after which content will be unavailable for viewing)

8. Select OK to save changes.

9. Exit Site Manager.

You edit channel rendering properties by specifying the default page, and identifying any scripts MCMS runs to process and render content.

Task 6-10. Modifying Channel Rendering Properties

1. Launch Site Manager and log on as channel manager.

2. Select the Channel icon to display the channel hierarchy.

3. Right-click the channel to edit and select Properties.

4. Select the Publishing tab.

5. In the Channel Rendering section, click Select.

6. Set options in the Default Page section of the Channel Rendering dialog box:

   • Choose Use First Page to render first page as default page for channel.

   • Choose Use page with This Name and type the name of the default page to specify first page.

7. Set options in the Channel Rendering section of the Channel Rendering dialog box:

   - Choose Script URL to Render Content

   - Use Channel Script with Pages (Yes—always run script/No—only run it on specified page)

   - Navigation URL to add navigational elements to pages

8. Returning to the Channel Rendering section of the Channel Properties dialog box, set the Apply to Descendants check box to apply these settings to all descendants of this channel.

9. Select OK to save changes.

10. Exit Site Manager.

You edit the Web Author default galleries by specifying the default location of template and resource galleries.

Task 6-11. Modifying Web Author Default Galleries

1. Launch Site Manager and log on as channel manager.

2. Select the Channel icon to display the channel hierarchy.

3. Right-click the channel to edit and select Properties.

4. Select the Web Authoring tab.

5. Select the location for storing the Web Author templates (browse in the Template Gallery box).

6. Select the location for storing the Web Author resources (browse in the Resource Gallery box).

7. Select OK to save changes.

8. Exit Site Manager.

You can change the organization of an existing channel hierarchy by sorting the pages within the channel.

Task 6-12. Sorting Channel Structure

1. Launch Site Manager and log on as channel manager.

2. Select the Channel icon to display the channel hierarchy.

3. Right-click the channel to edit and select Properties.

4. Select the Sorting tab on the Properties dialog box.

5. Select the item to move up or down in the sort list.

6. Select Up or Down to execute the move.

7. Select OK to save changes.

8. Exit Site Manager.

You can edit rights after a channel has been created.

Task 6-13. Modifying Channel Rights

1. Launch Site Manager and log on as channel manager.

2. Select the Channel icon to display the channel hierarchy.

3. Right-click the channel to edit and select Properties.

4. On the Rights tab, select Modify.

5. Next to Look in, select the user role from the drop-down list in the Select User Rights for Your New Channel dialog box.

6. Select the desired rights group and choose Add. Alternatively, select Add Parent's Rights to assign the same rights groups as the parent.

7. Select OK to save changes.

8. Exit Site Manager.

You can customize an existing channel by adding custom properties.

Task 6-14. Customizing Channels

1. Launch Site Manager and log on as channel manager.

2. Select the Channel icon to display the channel hierarchy.

3. Right-click the channel to edit and select Properties.

4. Select the Custom tab and choose New.

5. Set options in the Add Custom Property dialog box:

   - Name custom property

   - Select property type from drop-down (Text or Selection)

   - Enter text for custom Text property, or values for custom Selection property

6. Select OK to save changes.

7. Exit Site Manager.

You can copy or move an entire channel and its contents using cut and paste.

Task 6-15. Copying/Moving Channels

1. Launch Site Manager and log on as channel manager.
2. Select the Channel icon to display the channel hierarchy.
3. Right-click the source channel to view the context menu.
4. Select Copy (or Cut) to place a copy of the channel on the clipboard (using Cut causes the channel to be deleted after pasting to the new location).
5. Use the channel hierarchy to select the target location; select Paste to paste the channel from the clipboard.

Only administrators, channel managers, and template designers can delete and restore channels. When you delete a channel, it goes to the Deleted Items container.

Task 6-16. Deleting/Restoring Channels

1. Launch Site Manager and log on as channel manager.
2. Select the Channel icon to display the channel hierarchy.
3. Right-click the channel to delete.
4. Select Delete to move the channel to the Deleted Items container.
5. To restore the channel, expand Deleted Items, and move the channel back into the channel hierarchy.

Items moved to the Deleted Items container are no longer used in the MCMS container hierarchy, but remain in the database. To delete an item from the database and remove it permanently, the item must be removed from the Deleted Items container.

Task 6-17. Removing Channels

1. Launch Site Manager and log on as channel manager.
2. Select the Channel icon to display the channel hierarchy.
3. To completely remove one channel, expand Deleted Items, right-click the channel, and select Delete.
4. To completely remove all deleted channels, right-click Deleted Items and select Clear Deleted Items.

Managing Pages

You can copy or move pages among channels.

Task 6-18. Copying/Moving Pages

1. Launch Site Manager and log on as channel manager.

2. Select the Channel icon to display the channel hierarchy.

3. Right-click the channel containing the page to copy or move, and then select the page.

4. Select Copy to place a copy of the gallery on the clipboard (or Cut to move the gallery to the clipboard).

5. Use the channel hierarchy to select the destination; select Paste to add the gallery from the clipboard.

Only administrators, channel managers, and template designers can delete and restore pages from a channel. When you delete a page from a channel, it goes to the Deleted Items container.

Task 6-19. Deleting/Restoring Pages

1. Launch Site Manager and log on as channel manager.

2. Select the Channel icon to display the channel hierarchy.

3. Select the channel that contains the page to delete, and then select the items.

4. Select Delete to move items to the Deleted Items container.

5. To restore a page, move it from the Deleted Items container back into the channel hierarchy.

Removing a page deletes it permanently from the system. A page must be deleted before it can be permanently removed.

Task 6-20. Removing Pages

1. Launch Site Manager and log on as channel manager.

2. Select the Channels icon to display the channel hierarchy.

3. Expand Deleted Items, and remove the page using Delete.

Publishing new versions of pages that supersede the original (called *consecutive publication*) can be set up to switch over on a specified date. The consecutive pages must be in the same channel.

Task 6-21. Publishing Pages Consecutively

1. Launch Site Manager and log on as channel manager.

2. Select the Channels icon to display the channel hierarchy.

3. Expand the channel with the pages to be superseded.

4. Name the replacement page the same name as the original.

5. Set the expiration date of the original page to the replacement date.

6. Set the start date of the new page to the date on which you want the original page to be replaced (same date).

Both appear in the channel hierarchy with the same name. After an expiration date has been reached, the original page is removed. Page approval process (for each page) is independent. Obviously, pages should be approved before they go live; however, approval of each page version can be completed at any time.

You can publish channels consecutively as well. Superseding channel version may also be set to switch on a specified date.

Task 6-22. Publishing Channels Consecutively

1. Name the superseding channel the same name as the original channel.

2. Set the expiration date of the original channel to the replacement date.

3. Set the start date of the new channel to the same date as the original to be replaced.

If both channels share the same publishing dates, both appear in the channel hierarchy with the same name. Published channels that are children of an expired channel or are children of a channel with a start date in the future do not appear in the channel hierarchy.

Resource Galleries

Resource galleries hold the media—the images, audio files, and videos—that authors include with textual content. A resource manager is responsible for maintaining resource galleries via the Site Manager.

A resource manager's responsibilities generally go beyond copying files into cubbyholes in the container hierarchy. Often resources require special preparation for use in channels, whether it be encoding the video files with specific codecs, the color depth and image attributes of graphics, or the quality of the audio. An example of a different kind of special processing is found in the training industry—a bastion of MCMS applications. An important move afoot in the training industry is to create SCORM-compliant (Sharable Content Object Reference Model) *Sharable Content Resources*. To create these resources, you must create an XML wrapper to identify the actual content file. A resource manager should do this.

Managing Resource Galleries

This section describes how to create and maintain resource galleries so they facilitate authoring activities. Creating a resource gallery requires naming it and providing a description.

Task 6-23. Creating Resource Galleries

1. Launch Site Manager and log on as administrator or template designer.

2. Select the Resource Gallery icon to display the resource gallery hierarchy.

3. Use the resource gallery hierarchy to locate where the resource gallery is to be created.

4. Select the location for the new resource gallery. Right-click, select New, and then select Gallery.

5. Set the gallery properties in the New Resource Gallery dialog box:

   • Name (a descriptive name related to the resources contained within the gallery)

   • Description (maximum 255 characters)

6. Select OK to save changes.

7. Exit Site Manager.

After you have finished creating containers and rights groups, if necessary, assign groups to the containers.

Note If you have not created rights groups yet, refer to Chapter 5.

Task 6-24. Assigning Rights Groups to Resource Galleries

1. Launch Site Manager and log on as administrator or template designer.

2. Select the Resource Gallery icon to display the resource gallery hierarchy.

3. While you are creating a new gallery, click Select in the New Resource Gallery dialog box.

4. Next to Look in, select the user role from the drop-down list in the Select User Rights for Your New Resource Gallery dialog box.

5. Select the desired rights group and choose Add. Alternatively, select Add next to Add Rights Groups from Parent Containers to assign the same rights groups as the parent.

6. Select OK to save changes.

7. Exit Site Manager.

You can rename and modify a description of a resource gallery.

Task 6-25. Renaming/Modifying Descriptions of Resource Galleries

1. Launch Site Manager and log on as administrator or template designer.

2. Select the Gallery icon to display the resource gallery hierarchy.

3. Right-click the resource gallery, and select Rename.

4. Enter a name and press Enter to save changes.

5. Right-click the resource gallery, and select Properties.

6. Edit the Description (maximum of 255 characters).

7. Exit the Site Manager.

You will undoubtedly need to edit a gallery's rights.

Task 6-26. Modifying Rights for Resource Galleries

1. Launch Site Manager and log on as administrator or template designer.

2. Select the Resource Gallery icon to display the resource gallery hierarchy.

3. Right-click the resource gallery and select Properties.

4. On the Rights Tab, select Modify.

5. Next to Look in, select the user role from the drop-down list in the Select User Rights for Your New Resource Gallery dialog box.

6. Select the desired rights group and choose Add. Alternatively, select Add next to Add Rights Groups from Parent Containers to assign the same rights groups as the parent.

7. Select OK to save changes.

8. Exit Site Manager.

You can copy or move a resource gallery.

Task 6-27. Copying/Moving Resource Galleries

1. Launch Site Manager and log on as administrator or template designer.

2. Select the Resource Gallery icon to display the resource gallery hierarchy.

3. Right-click the source resource gallery to view the context menu.

4. Select Copy (or Cut) to place a copy of the resource gallery on the clipboard. Using Cut causes the resource gallery to be deleted after pasting to the new location.

5. Use the resource gallery hierarchy to select the target location; select Paste to paste the resource gallery from the clipboard.

Task 6-28. Deleting/Restoring Resource Galleries as Administrator or Template Designer

1. Launch Site Manager and log on as administrator or template designer.

2. Select the Resource Gallery icon to display the resource gallery hierarchy.

3. Right-click the resource gallery to delete.

4. Select Delete to move the resource gallery to the Deleted Items container.

5. To restore the resource gallery, expand Deleted Items, and move the resource gallery back into the resource gallery hierarchy.

Items moved to Deleted Items no longer show up in the gallery hierarchy, but remain in the MCMS database. Remove an item by removing it from Deleted Items.

Task 6-29. Removing Resource Galleries

1. Launch Site Manager and log on as administrator or template designer.

2. Select the Resource Gallery icon to display the resource gallery hierarchy.

3. To completely remove one resource gallery, expand Deleted Items, right-click the resource gallery, and select Delete.

4. To completely remove all deleted resource galleries (and the resources, too), right-click Deleted Items and select Clear Deleted Items.

Managing Resources

You can copy or move a resource from the resource gallery.

Task 6-30. Copying/Moving Resources from Galleries

1. Launch Site Manager and log on as administrator or template designer.

2. Select the Resource Gallery icon to display the resource gallery hierarchy.

3. Select the resource gallery containing the resource (or resources) that you want to copy or move.

4. Right-click the resource to copy or move to view the context menu.

5. Select Copy (or Cut) to place a copy of the resource on the clipboard. Using Cut causes the resource to be deleted after pasting to the new location.

6. Use the resource gallery hierarchy to select the target location; select Paste to paste the resource from the clipboard.

Only administrators, resource managers, and template designers can delete and restore files (resources) from a resource gallery.

Task 6-31. Deleting/Restoring Resources from Galleries

1. Launch Site Manager and log on as an administrator.

2. Select the Resource Gallery icon to display the resource gallery hierarchy.

3. Select the gallery that contains the resource (or resources) to delete.

4. Select the resource(s) to delete, and then right-click the resource(s) to view the context menu.

5. Select Delete to move the resource to the Deleted Items container.

6. To restore the resource, expand Deleted Items, and move the resource back into the resource gallery hierarchy.

Items moved to Deleted Items no longer show up in the resource gallery hierarchy, but remain in the MCMS database. To remove it permanently, remove it from Deleted Items.

Task 6-32. Removing Resources

1. Launch Site Manager and log on as resource manager.

2. Select the Resource Gallery icon to display the resource gallery hierarchy.

3. To completely remove one resource, expand Deleted Items, right-click the resource, and select Delete.

4. To completely remove all deleted resources (and resource galleries, too), right-click Deleted Items and select Clear Deleted Items.

Templates

The intent of an MCMS site is to empower information workers to collaborate and create their own portal. Distributing the IT load makes sense and placing control of the information in the hands of those who use it makes even more sense. This can be an efficient strategy if the publication system makes sense, too. Templates are a large part of the strategy because they enable business-oriented content contributors not only to focus on but also to understand site content more thoroughly. In this model, template design is also a collaborative process between Web developers and the information architects who analyze the logic and presentation of business data.

For the MCMS publication administrator, two masters are served: The template management process should provide fingertip access to content contributors and promote innovation at the design end. Create your publication system so the correct template for a job is always a clear choice. Template clutter should be minimized—on the page and in the portal workspace. Designers should work in an environment where preconfigured blocks of information and tools are available and their output can be tested before it goes live.

Managing Templates with Galleries

Galleries serve two functions: They provide authors access to appropriate templates and they provide administrators a way to store and organize templates. This section of procedures describes how to create template galleries and how to assign access to rights groups. You manage galleries in much the same way you manage files in any Windows environment.

When you create a template gallery for the first time, you need to name it and provide a description of up to a maximum of 255 characters. Describe content or rights groups using templates in the gallery.

Task 6-33. Creating a Template Gallery

1. Launch Site Manager and log on as template designer.

2. Select the Gallery icon to display the gallery hierarchy.

3. Select the location for the new Template Gallery. Right-click, select New, and then select Gallery.

4. Set the gallery properties in the New Template Gallery dialog box:

   • Name (a descriptive name related to the templates contained within the gallery)

   • Description (maximum 255 characters)

5. Select OK to save changes.

6. Exit Site Manager.

After a template gallery has been created, rights groups need access so they can use or modify them. Before we proceed to that task, however, let's examine some gallery administration chores.

Task 6-34. Modifying Gallery Names/Descriptions

1. Launch Site Manager and log on as template designer.

2. Select the Gallery icon to display the gallery hierarchy.

3. Right-click the template gallery and select Rename.

4. Enter the name and press Enter to save changes.

5. Right-click the template gallery, and select Properties.

6. Edit the Description (maximum of 255 characters).

7. Exit the Site Manager.

Note You can't edit the channel name, although it appears on the General tab of the Properties dialog box.

Managing Gallery Rights

Assigning rights groups to a template gallery allows members of the group access to its contents.

Note   Refer to Chapter 5 for the procedure to create rights groups.

Task 6-35. Assigning Rights Groups to Template Galleries

1. Launch Site Manager and log on as template designer.

2. Select the Template Gallery icon to display the template gallery hierarchy.

3. While you are creating a new template gallery, click Select in the New Template Gallery dialog box.

4. Next to Look in, select the user role from the drop-down list in the Select User Rights for Your New Template Gallery dialog box.

5. Select the desired rights group and choose Add. Alternatively, select Add next to Add Rights Groups from Parent Containers to assign the same rights groups as the parent.

6. Select OK to save changes.

7. Exit Site Manager.

After the gallery has been created and assigned a rights group, you can edit roles and rights.

Task 6-36. Modifying Rights for the Gallery

1. Launch Site Manager and log on as template designer.

2. Select the Template Gallery icon to display galleries.

3. Right-click the template gallery and select Properties.

4. On the Rights tab, select Modify.

5. Next to Look in, select the user role from the drop-down list in the Select User Rights for Your New Template Gallery dialog box.

6. Select the desired rights group and choose Add. Alternatively, select Add next to Add Rights Groups from Parent Containers to assign the same rights groups as the parent.

7. Select OK to save changes.

8. Exit Site Manager.

Copying and Moving Galleries

You can copy or move a gallery easily.

Task 6-37. Copying/Moving a Gallery

1. Launch Site Manager and log on as template designer.

2. Select the Template Gallery icon to display galleries.

3. Right-click the source template gallery to view the context menu.

4. Select Copy (or Cut) to place a copy of the gallery on the clipboard. Using Cut causes the template gallery to be deleted after pasting to the new location.

5. Use the template gallery hierarchy to select the target location; select Paste to paste the template gallery from the clipboard.

Deleting and Restoring Galleries

Administrators, channel managers, and template designers can delete and restore template galleries. Deleting a gallery moves it to the Deleted Items container.

Task 6-38. Deleting/Restoring a Gallery

1. Launch Site Manager and log on as template designer.

2. Select the Template Gallery icon to display galleries.

3. Right-click the template gallery to delete.

4. Select Delete to move items to the Deleted Items container.

5. To restore the gallery, expand Deleted Items, and move the item back into the gallery hierarchy.

Items moved to Deleted Items no longer show up in the gallery hierarchy, but remain in the MCMS database. Remove an item by removing it from Deleted Items.

Task 6-39. Removing a Gallery

1. Launch Site Manager and log on as template designer.

2. Select the Template Gallery icon to display galleries.

3. To completely remove one template gallery, expand Deleted Items, right-click the template gallery, and select Delete.

4. To completely remove all deleted template galleries (and templates, too), right-click Deleted Items and select Clear Deleted Items.

Managing Templates

The tendency is to think of templates as crystalline boilerplate—once they're in place, they don't change. Templates facilitate reuse, but they also facilitate access because they maintain consistency and cogently represent a user's expectations about the content. Much of the logic and the emotional appeal of your site is provided by the organizational scheme created by templates. Whether your templates are stable or constantly changing depends upon the nature of your business. You should expect that templates are going to evolve regularly and you should plan a template strategy. The following are the procedural "tactics" for template administration.

Task 6-40. Deleting/Restoring Templates from Galleries

1. Launch Site Manager and log on as template designer.

2. Select the Template Gallery icon to display galleries.

3. Select the gallery that contains template (or templates) to delete, and then select the items.

4. Select the template(s) to delete, right-click the template(s) to view the context menu.

5. Select Delete to move items to the Deleted Items container.

6. To restore the template, move it from the Deleted Items container back into the template gallery hierarchy.

Items moved to the Deleted Items no longer show up in the resource gallery hierarchy, but remain in the MCMS database. To remove items permanently, remove them from Deleted Items.

Task 6-41. Removing Templates

1. Launch Site Manager and log on as template designer.

2. Select the Template Gallery icon to display galleries.

3. To completely remove one template, expand Deleted Items, right-click the template, and select Delete.

4. To completely remove all deleted templates (and template galleries, too), right-click Deleted Items and select Clear Deleted Items.

Note Administrators, channel managers, and template designers can delete and restore. Deleted items are kept in the Deleted Items container.

If you make changes to a template, you may decide to revert to a previous version or another template, for example, that was previously approved.

Task 6-42. Reverting to the Last Approved Template

1. Launch Site Manager and log on as template designer.

2. Select the Template Gallery icon to display galleries.

3. Select the template gallery containing the template from which you want to revert to the last approved version.

4. Right-click the template to view the context menu.

5. Select Revert to Approved.

If there are changes to be made in a template that may affect individual pages differently, you can search for all pages that use the same template by creating a dependent report.

Task 6-43. Identifying Pages That Use a Particular Template

1. Launch Site Manager and log on as template designer.

2. Select the Template Gallery icon to display galleries.

3. Select the template gallery containing the template for which you want to find dependent pages (client pages that use this template).

4. Right-click the template to view the context menu.

5. Select Dependent Report.

Summary

The Site Manager is the tool used by administrators to manage the publication environment. With it you can create and manage rights groups and channels. As authors create pages to put in the various channel containers, the administrator approves them to be viewed on the live site.

The administrator also provides resource containers to make media resources available to authors in their pages.

CHAPTER 7

■■■

Deploying Content

This chapter covers

- Exporting dynamic content objects
- Importing channel and rights objects
- Importing templates and resources
- Tracking revisions
    - Revision histories
    - Clearing revisions by timestamp
- Using Site Stager
    - `Destination` directories
    - Granting access to the staging computers

Deployment is the replication of objects from a development or authoring environment into a testing or production environment. Only content managed by MCMS can be deployed using the procedures outlined in this chapter. Web elements that are not based on data from the Content Repository, such as ASPX scripts, must be deployed using different methods (either by hand or programmatically). Microsoft recommends its Applications Server for the job; however, this is outside the scope of this book.

Deployment can be done as a full or incremental replication. Typically a systems administrator deploys a full site using the Site Manager UI. Incremental deployment is performed using COM-based scripts. This chapter covers using Site Manager to perform deployments.

Deployment occurs when content is replicated to the target environment (typically a production server) via packages of XML and resources. Figure 7-1 illustrates MCMS's two *full deployment* options: Site Manager (deploys dynamic content) and Site Stager (converts dynamic content into static HTML).

It is recommended that as much as possible, content should remain dynamic because it's more easily modified and personalized.

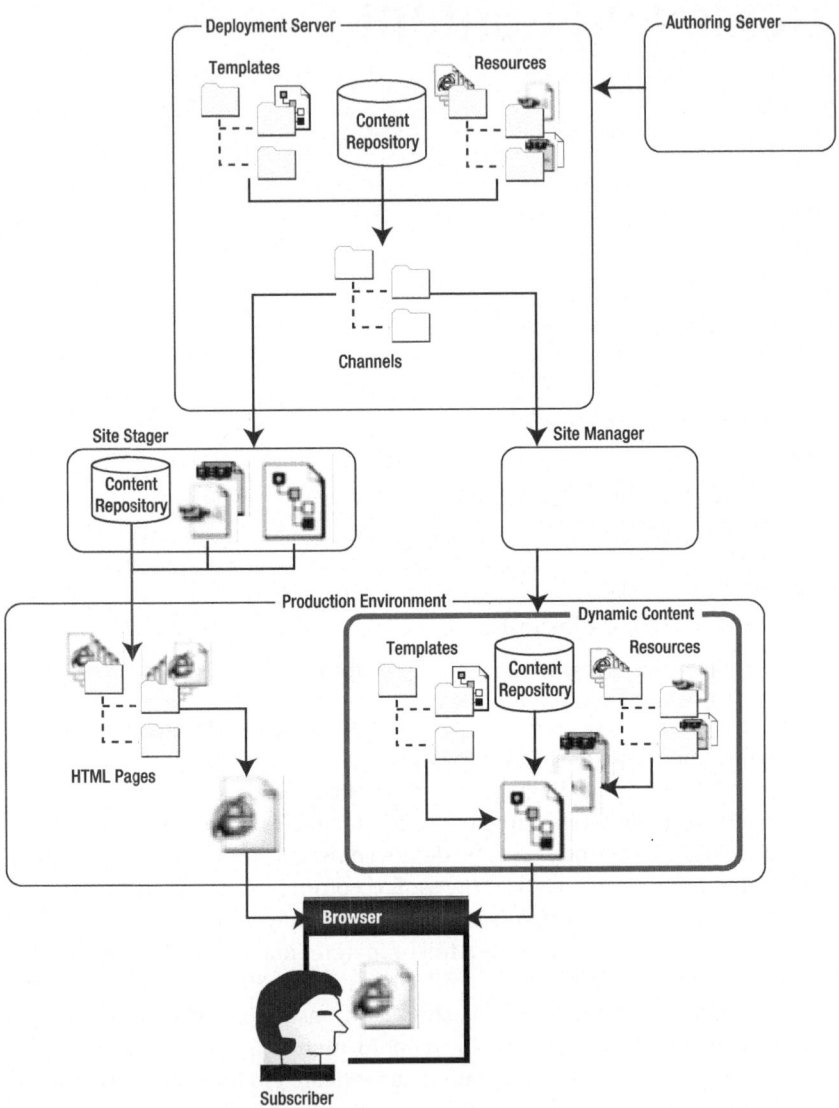

Figure 7-1. Deployment options

An administrator uses Site Manager to export objects from the deployment (source) server and import them to the production environment (destination server). Those objects include the following:

- Containers (channels, galleries, or rights groups)

- Pages, resources, templates, or users

- Site deployment objects (packages containing the imported and exported objects)

Note For additional information about deployment, refer to `http://www.microsoft.com/cmserver/default.aspx?url=/cmserver/techinfo/deployment/default.htm`.

Exporting Dynamic Content Objects

Exporting requires administrative permissions. Containers (channel, gallery, or user role) or individual items (page, resource, template, or rights group) can be exported.

Task 7-1. Setting Export Options

1. Launch the Site Manager, log on as an administrator, and select Start.

2. Choose Tools ➤ Options. In the Export Package Defaults section:

   - Set or clear the Enable Limited Export Notice check box.

   - Set or clear Enable Expanded Export Notice check box.

   - Set or clear Enable Preview Export Prompt for Confirmation During Export check box.

3. Select OK to save changes and exit.

The default behavior is to include all the contents of any container for export. Child objects (containers) are included by default unless they are explicitly selected for exclusion. Dependent objects of included objects must be included. Parent containers of included objects (containers) are not included for export by default.

Task 7-2. Excluding Objects from Exports

1. Launch the Site Manager, log on as an administrator, and select Start.

2. Choose File ➤ Package ➤ Export to open the Site Deployment Export dialog box.

3. In the All Containers window, select one or more of the Channel, Subchannel, Resource Gallery or Resource, or Template Gallery or Template objects, and then select Include. The selected objects are displayed in the Included and Excluded Export Objects window.

4. Again in the All Containers window, select the object to be specifically excluded from the export. This may be an individual subchannel, page, resource, or template that typically has been automatically included by virtue of its parent being included. Select the desired item and click the Include button again.

5. In the Included and Excluded Export Objects window, select the item(s) to be specifically excluded and click the Exclude button. An X should appear next to the excluded items.

6. If an item has been included or excluded, and is no longer required to be part of the export process, select the item and click the Remove button.

You also need to create or export rights groups and members so users have the appropriate rights to access content. Make sure the members of exported rights groups have accounts on the destination system's domain. Without accounts on the target domain, users will not have access to imported objects. Microsoft recommends that you do not export users when the source and target servers are not on a domain (or are on domains that have trusted domain relationships).

Task 7-3. Exporting Rights Groups and Users

1. Launch the Site Manager, log on as an administrator, and select Start.

2. Choose File ➤ Package ➤ Export to open the Site Deployment Export dialog box.

   • On the Rights Options tab, select the Export Rights Groups check box to export the rights groups. This also enables Export Users to be unselected, so that the users assigned to the exported containers are specifically not included in the export.

   • To include the users with the exported rights groups, select the Export Users check box.

Before exporting, you can preview what MCMS thinks you have selected for export.

Task 7-4. Viewing or Printing the Export Preview Report

1. Launch the Site Manager, log on as an administrator, and select Start.

2. Choose File ➤ Package ➤ Export to open the Site Deployment Export dialog box.

3. Select Report and Export Preview. A new Export Preview Report is displayed.

4. To print, select File ➤ Print.

5. To exit, select File ➤ Close.

You should compare the Export Preview Report to the Export Report for any discrepancies.

Task 7-5. Executing the Export

1. Launch the Site Manager, log on as an administrator, and select Start.

2. Choose File ➤ Package ➤ Export. This displays the Site Deployment Export dialog box.

3. On the Item Selection tab, select any of the MCMS containers or objects to export.

Note To export only the containers (for example, the Resource Galleries, but not the resources inside), set the Export Containers Only check box.

4. Generate an Export Preview Report by choosing Report ➤ Export Preview. Review and reconcile this report against what you have specifically selected for export. Revise the selections, if required.

5. Next to Export to File (.sdo), enter the desired path and file name of the exported objects. It is not necessary to add the extension .sdo. You can click the Browse button to navigate to a specific directory to contain the new export file.

6. When you're satisfied that the appropriate items have been selected for export, click the Export button in the lower-right corner to begin the export process. If you didn't preview the export configuration, a dialog box may appear offering you the opportunity to do so now.

7. On the dialog box that appears indicating that the export is complete, click the Show button to view the Export Report. Print the Export Report and reconcile it against the Export Preview Report to verify expected results.

8. Select OK to complete the export process.

9. If desired, you can save this set of items to export as an Export Profile. On the Site Deployment Export dialog box, select File and Save Export Profile (As) and enter a path and file name. This MCMS Site Deployment Export Profile file will have an extension of .sde.

■**Note** The Export Completed dialog box indicates that the object file was created successfully. An error message is posted if the export is unsuccessful. You can cancel an export operation at any time; however, the Cancel command may not execute immediately.

To view or print a report of items exported via the MCMS Site Manager, you must request the report during the export process.

Importing Channel and Rights Objects

The import process affects not only the channel container hierarchy, but also the Content Repository. For this reason, it is highly recommended that the SQL Server database be backed up immediately prior to importation to prevent data loss.

■**Tip** For additional information about SQL Server backup and restore, refer to http:// go.microsoft.com/fwlink/?LinkId=9559.

System administrator credentials are required to manage importing objects. Channel import objects include containers (channels, galleries, or rights group roles) or items (pages, resources, templates, or rights groups).

When importing items into an MCMS site, three sets of configuration options are available as tabs on the Site Deployment Import dialog box:

- Container Rules
- Rights Groups
- Orphaned Objects

Task 7-6. Configuring Container Rules

1. Launch the Site Manager, and log on as system administrator.

2. Select File ➤ Package ➤ Import. The Site Deployment Import dialog box opens.

   You can add new containers or replace existing containers. There are separate configuration rules to set for each procedure.

3. To add containers, select the Container Rules tab and choose one of the following options in Adding Containers:

- Select the Inherit Parent Rights option to maintain the current security policies. (Imported containers inherit parent container privileges; assigned rights group are removed if they are not present on the import server.)

- Select the Package Rights option to retain security settings and rights groups assigned on the source server (only if the rights were actually exported).

- Select the Leave Rights List Empty option to import objects with no access rights.

4. To replace containers, select one of the following options:

   - Select the Inherit Parent Rights option to grant replaced containers the users assigned to the destination parent container.

   - Select the Replace with Package Rights option to retain security settings and rights groups assigned on the source server (only if the rights were actually exported).

   - Select the Keep Destination Rights option to replace containers, but maintain the original destination rights groups.

   - Select the Combine Package and Destination Rights option to import containers and add their rights group(s) to the existing rights groups on the destination server.

5. To modify the container hierarchy, select one or both of the following from the Container Rules tab:

   - Select the Change Container Hierarchy on Destination to Match the Package Hierarchy check box to maintain the hierarchy from the export server.

   - Select the Delete All Existing Container Contents When Replacing a Container check box to delete all contained content before containers and their children are imported.

Note Templates can't be deleted if pages based on the template still exist.

After you have imported a container hierarchy, you need to import or configure rights groups and members. Use the Export Report to examine the rights groups to use for container mapping. Rights groups are imported with or without members. Newly imported members require domain accounts to be authenticated on the import system.

The import from file (with an .sdo extension) should be the same for containers, rights groups, and orphaned objects.

Task 7-7. Configuring Rights Groups for Import

1. If the Site Deployment Import dialog box is not displayed, launch the Site Manager, and log on as system administrator.

2. Select File ➤ Package ➤ Import.

3. In the "Select How Rights Groups Are Imported" section of the Rights Group tab, select one of the following options:

   - Select the Do Not Import Any Rights Groups or Users option to prevent the import of rights groups and users.

   - Select the Import User Rights Groups option to enable rights groups import.

   - Select the Import User Rights Groups and Users option to enable group and user import. If this option is selected, the Select How Users Are Imported section is enabled.

4. If the Select How Users Are Imported section is enabled, select one of the following options:

   - Select the Use Only the Package User Lists option to add users to replace rights groups. (Duplicate rights groups member lists are overwritten.)

   - Select the Use Package and Destination User Lists, Combining Them for Replaced Rights Groups option to add the users in the object file. (Duplicate rights groups member lists are merged.)

■**Note** If no rights groups are contained in the import package (because they were not exported), the only option available is the Do Not Import Any Rights Groups of Users option.

Task 7-8. Selecting an Orphaned Objects Container

1. If the Site Deployment Import dialog box is not displayed, launch the Site Manager, and log on as system administrator.

2. Select File ➤ Package ➤ Import.

3. On the Orphaned Objects tab, set the default container location where containers and objects that no longer have parents (orphans) are imported. Browse to select the default orphaned-objects container. Separate locations can be specified for channels, resources, Resource Galleries, templates, and Template Galleries.

If a default Orphaned Objects container is not specified, it is automatically created during import (CMS Default Site Deploy Destination). Default

Orphaned Objects containers are created for channels, Template Galleries, and Resource Galleries.

A list of containers, rights groups, and orphaned objects is saved in an import profile. You can open an import profile and print a report of its contents.

Task 7-9. Generating an Import Report

1. Launch the Site Manager, and log on as system administrator.

2. Select File ➤ Package ➤ Import.

3. Select Report ➤ Import Preview to open the Import dialog box.

4. Select File ➤ Print.

5. Select Save Import Profile As and enter the profile name (saved with the `.sdi` extension).

Import Preview Reports are often time consuming to generate. A progress indicator is posted when Import Preview is selected.

After importation begins, it cannot be stopped, although it can be rolled back if the import system has been backed up (including the Content Repository).

Task 7-10. Executing the Import Process/Viewing Reports

1. Launch the Site Manager, and log on as system administrator.

2. Select File ➤ Package ➤ Import.

3. The Import confirmation dialog box appears when a successful import is completed. An error message is displayed upon an unsuccessful attempt.

4. In the Import confirmation dialog box, select Show Report to view the Import Report.

The Import Report lists containers and items modified during import, including deleted objects and broken links.

Importing Templates and Resources

Back up your server before importing templates and resources. When importing templates, referenced files must be imported, including

- Templates
- Frameset pages (headers, footers, logo pages, and so on)

- External files referenced by relative URLs
- Virtual directories (if templates reference IIS virtual directories)
- Cascading style sheets (CSS)
- Files referenced in scripts (ASP, VB Script, Jscript, and JavaScript source files, links, and include files)

Tracking Revisions

MCMS tracks revisions to page content and resources used on pages. Using revision tracking, administrators can compare various approved versions of a page. Revisions apply to page content and resources only—not channels or templates.

Template scripts (`.asp` and `.aspx` files) are not versioned. To version scripts, use Visual Studio .NET and Visual SourceSafe.

A *revision* is a duplicate page object stored in the Content Repository, created when the content is modified and/or re-approved. Revision tracking is under administrative control with the following characteristics:

- Enabled by default.
- Can't be turned off.
- Versions are only limited by the size of the database.
- No option is available to automatically delete versions or to stop the creation of new versions.

Although versions don't consume significant system resources, large individual resources undergoing frequent revisions can cause the tracking database to grow in size because each copy remains in the database.

Revision Histories

Revision histories pertain to pages and resources that have been modified and approved. Revision histories are not exported.

Unapproved page revisions provide the following:

- Date/time of the last modification
- Status

Approved revisions provide the following:

- Date/time of the initial approval or date/time of the initial resource creation
- Type (page or resource)
- Name of person who approved the revision

Connected pages use the same template or use templates from a set of connected templates. The revision history for connected pages is saved in the revision history of the corresponding connected pages and templates. When MCMS deploys content, the revision history of a page reflects changes to each MCMS object that is associated with that page.

Clearing Revisions by Timestamp

Revisions made before a specified date and time can be deleted. The default value for the date is three months (prior). Revisions are deleted from the entire site.

Task 7-11. Clearing Revisions by Timestamp

1. Launch the Site Manager, and log on as system administrator.

2. Select Tools ➤ Clear Revision History.

3. In the Clear Revisions dialog box, select the month, day, and time (revisions approved before the selected date will be cleared).

4. Select Clear to confirm the revision history clear operation.

Revisions made before the date and time you specified are deleted.

Using Site Stager

An administrator uses Site Stager to convert dynamic sites into static HTML pages, including navigation links. Use Site Stager to create staging *profiles*, which contain the information required to stage the site:

- Unique name
- Root directory of staged site
- Channels to be staged
- Schedule for staging (duration between staging versions)

Multiple sites can be staged from the same source server by creating a unique profile for each site. Staging maintains channel security.

Site Stager will convert ASP-based sites, but will not stage ASP.NET-based sites. Site Stager will deploy content on any Web server.

The MCMS Site Stager application must be installed on the source server and access must be granted to the target (staged) computer. Chapter 2 provides additional information about installing MCMS and granting access.

Destination Directories

Site Stager crawls the dynamic MCMS site, converting pages to static HTML files and linked resources, outputting them into a directory structure that is identical to the channel hierarchy. Site Stager organizes these files and folders under a root directory named Destination directories. In addition to the Channel folder, Destination directories contains additional subdirectories:

- **Logs:** Stores log files (can be opened with a text editor) that contain descriptions of events (file downloads, folder creation, and so on); used internally by Site Stager.

- **Temp:** Temporary storage for files during the staging process.

- **Resources:** Stores externally referenced resources.

- **Channels:** Stores staged HTML content.

The files and folders under Destination directories may not be removed or altered.

If you reference resources externally to the channel hierarchy, you must create a virtual path to this directory so Site Stager can make the contents available.

A log file is created whenever Site Stager executes a profile, whether manually or programmatically. Staging errors are recorded in log files. The default folder location is

```
C:\Program Files\Microsoft Content Management Server\
Site Stager\SiteStagerLogs
```

To provide a unique name, the date, time, and GUID are appended to the log file name:

```
profile name_year_month_day_hours_minutes_seconds_ {GUID}.log
```

Granting Access to the Staging Computers

The MCMS root staging (NR/System/Staging IIS) virtual directory is globally accessible by default and poses a significant security risk. Microsoft recommends that you restrict access to remote staging computers.

Task 7-12. Granting Access to the Staging Computer

1. Launch the Internet Services Manager.

2. Expand Default Web Site, NR, System, and then select the Staging folder. View Properties.

3. Edit the IP address and domain name restrictions on the Directory Security tab of the Staging Properties dialog box as follows.

4. In the IP Address and Domain Name Restrictions dialog box, do the following:

- Select the IP address for the computer where Site Stager is installed (if the address is listed)

Or

- Select Add (if the address is not listed) and complete the dialog box.

- Select the Type of IP Address (Single Computer, Group of Computers, Domain Name).

- Enter the IP address.

- Identify the computer name associated with the IP address for the DNS lookup.

5. Save changes and close the Staging Properties dialog box.

After you grant access to staging computers, prepare the MCMS site for staging.

A profile can only stage channels for which a *stage-as* domain user account has been created and granted subscription rights. Stage-as user accounts support multiple staging profiles.

Task 7-13. Creating a Stage-As Domain User Account

1. Log on to the Windows NT domain controller as an administrator.

2. Launch Computer Management from Administrative Tools.

3. Expand Local Users and Groups, and select New User.

4. Enter account information in the New User dialog box:

- Enter a name: `<domain>\<stage-as user account name>`.

- Enter a password.

5. Save changes and exit the Computer Management dialog box.

Stage different versions of a site with individual stage-as accounts and profiles for each version. Microsoft recommends using stage-as user accounts for staging only.

The staged computer must have an administrator's user account on the Site Stager's domain, called the *destination user account*. This account must be granted Log On As Batch Job, Log On Locally, and write privileges in the `Destination` directory (and all subdirectories).

Task 7-14. Creating a Destination User Windows NT Domain User Account

1. Log on to the Windows NT domain controller as an administrator.

2. Launch Computer Management from Administrative Tools.

3. Expand Local Users and Groups, and select New User.

4. Enter account information in the New User dialog box:

   • Enter a name: `<domain>\<destination user account name>`.

   • Enter a password.

5. Save changes and exit the Computer Management dialog box.

Task 7-15. Adding a Destination User to Administrators

1. Log on to the Windows NT domain controller as an administrator.

2. Launch Computer Management from Administrative Tools.

3. Expand Local Users and Groups, and select Groups.

4. Select Administrators, and view Properties.

5. Select Add in the Administrators Properties dialog box.

6. Select the domain from the Select Users or Groups dialog box.

7. Select a name.

8. Select Add.

9. Save changes, and exit the Computer Management dialog box.

Log On As Batch Job rights are granted on the computer with Site Stager.

Task 7-16. Granting a Destination User Log On As Batch Job Rights

1. Launch Administrative Tools from the Control Panel on the Site Stager computer.

2. Select Local Security Policy from Administrative Tools.

3. Select IP Security Management.

4. Expand Local Policies, and select User Rights Assignment from the Local Security Settings.

5. Select Log On as Batch Job from the Policy list.

6. Select Add from the Local Security Policy Setting dialog box.

7. Edit the account information in the Select Users or Groups dialog box:

- Select the domain for the user account.
- Select the user account.

8. Select Add.

9. Save changes, and close the Select Users or Groups dialog box.

Task 7-17. Granting a Destination User Log On Locally Rights

1. Launch Administrative Tools from the Control Panel on the Site Stager computer.

2. Select Local Security Policy from Administrative Tools.

3. In the IP Security Management message box, click OK.

4. Expand Local Policies, and select User Rights Assignment from the Local Security Settings.

5. Select Log On Locally from the Policy list.

6. Select Add from the Local Security Policy Setting dialog box.

7. Select either the Users or Groups button and enter account information:

- Select the domain for the user account.
- Select the user account name.

8. Save changes, and close the Users or Groups dialog box.

Task 7-18. Configuring a Destination User Account on a Site Stager Computer

1. Launch the Site Stager, and log on as system administrator.

2. Choose OK to select Destination User Is Not a Member of the Administrators.

3. Choose OK to validate the selection in the Destination User Setup dialog box.

4. Select Configure.

5. Enter account information in the User Setup dialog box:

- Select Type <domain>\<user name>.
- Enter a password.

6. Save changes, and exit the dialog box.

The destination user account must be assigned appropriate rights before you can configure a stage-as user account.

Task 7-19. Creating a Subscriber Rights Group

1. Launch the Site Stager, and log on as the site manager.
2. Select Start.
3. Select User Roles (Site Manager).
4. Select New Rights Group (In Subscribers, User Roles).
5. Rename [New Rights Group] to Stage-As (Subscribers).
6. Save changes, and exit Site Stager.

Task 7-20. Creating a Resource Manager Rights Group

1. Launch the Site Stager, and log on as the site manager.
2. Select Start.
3. Select User Roles (Site Manager).
4. Select New Rights Group (In Resource Managers, User Roles).
5. Rename [New Rights Group] to Stage-As (Resource Managers).
6. Save changes, and exit Site Stager.

Task 7-21. Adding a Stage-As User Account as a Member of the Subscribers Rights Group

1. Launch the Site Stager, and log on as the site manager.
2. Select Start.
3. Select User Roles (Site Manager).
4. Select Stage-As (In Subscribers, User Roles); view Properties.
5. Rename [New Rights Group] to Stage-As (Subscribers).
6. Select Modify on the Group Members tab of the Stage-As Properties dialog box.
7. Select the domain in the Modify Members–Stage-As dialog box.
8. Select Users group in the Modify Members–Stage-As dialog box; select Members.
9. Select your account in the NT Group Members dialog box and verify your selection.
10. Save changes, and exit Site Stager.

Task 7-22. Adding a Stage-As User Account as a Member of the Resource Manager Rights Group

1. Launch the Site Manager, and log on as the site manager.

2. Select Start.

3. Select User Roles (Resource Managers).

4. Select Stage-As (In Resource Managers, User Roles); view Properties.

5. Select Modify in the Group Members tab of the Stage-As Properties dialog box.

6. Select the domain in the Modify Members–Stage-As dialog box.

7. Select the Users group in the Modify Members–Stage-As dialog box; select Members.

8. Select your account in the NT Group Members dialog box, and then verify your selection.

9. Save changes, and exit Site Stager.

Assign channel access to the Stage-As Subscriber rights group to enable the staging of the channel.

Task 7-23. Assigning Stage-As Rights Group Access Channels

1. Launch the Site Manager, and log on as the site manager.

2. Select Start.

3. Select the Channels icon to display the channels hierarchy.

4. Expand Channels, expand the MCMS site, select the channel to stage, and view Properties.

5. Select the Rights tab, and choose Modify.

6. Edit Stage-As Rights in the Select User Rights for Channel dialog box:

   - Select Subscribers, and Stage-As (rights group members).

   - Add the rights group to the channel.

7. Save changes, exit Site Stager.

Channel access must be granted for every channel to stage. Next a staging profile must be created.

Task 7-24. Creating a Staging Profile

1. Launch the Site Stager, and log on as the site manager.

2. Select Start.

3. Select Add in the Site Stager Administration dialog box.

4. Edit the staging profile properties:

   • Name the staging profile.

   • Select Active to enable automatic scheduling.

   • Enter the [domain\user name] for the Stage-As account.

   • Select the Users group from the Modify Members–Stage-As dialog box; select Members.

   • Enter a password.

   • Enter the default, top-level page for the staged site.

   • Enter the `Destination` directory or browse to select it.

   • Enter the path of the program (Shell After Staging) to be run after staging.

   • Enter a description for the profile.

5. Save changes, and exit Site Stager.

After you have configured the staging profile, you can schedule the execution.

Task 7-25. Scheduling Automated Staging

1. Launch the Site Stager, and log on as the site manager.

2. Select the profile to run from the Site Stager Administration dialog box.

3. Edit the scheduling properties in the Schedule tab:

   • Select the staging interval.

   • Enter the Start Time.

   • Set the schedule information for a selected interval.

4. Select Apply, verify the scheduler, and exit Site Stager.

Interval options include

• Daily

• Weekly

- Monthly
- Once
- At System Startup
- At Logon
- When Idle

The profile must be marked active to be staged automatically. Only one profile may be staged at a time to a `Destination` directory. If you are staging more than one profile to a `Destination` directory using the automated scheduler, ensure that they cannot run concurrently. Make sure there is enough unused space to accommodate both sets of staged pages.

Task 7-26. Staging a Site Manually

1. Launch the Site Stager, and log on as the site manager.

2. Select the profile to stage in the Site Stager Administration dialog box.

3. Select Stage Now.

4. Exit Site Stager.

Even when it is closed, Site Stager continues as a background task until it completes. If errors occur during staging, they're written to the log. Site Stager terminates execution after all channels have been converted.

Summary

MCMS content can be deployed using the MCMS Site Manager. Administrator rights are required. This content is easily exported from a source server into a single file and can subsequently be imported into a destination server. The granularity of export and import options facilitates a flexible deployment process.

MCMS content includes channels, subchannels and pages, resources and Resource Galleries, templates and Template Galleries, as well as rights groups and users.

Site staging is not possible for ASP.NET-based sites. Site staging is only possible for MCMS ASP-based sites. MCMS sites built today are typically ASP.NET-based sites, rendering the current MCMS Site Stager functionality unusable.

■ ■ ■

CHAPTER 8

Troubleshooting

This chapter covers

- Troubleshooting installation and configuration
  - If setup was unsuccessful
  - Upgrading from MCMS 2000 to MCMS 2002
  - Uninstalling MCMS 2002
  - MCMS 2002 Standard Edition
  - SQL Server database issues
  - Windows Server 2003 and MCMS 2002
- Using MCMS administrative tools
  - Site Manager
  - Site Stager
- Supporting authors
- Dealing with Visual Studio .NET issues

This chapter primarily addresses troubleshooting configuration and administration issues. Wherever possible, solutions to problems and references to additional information are provided. Some debugging tips and techniques are listed in the areas where they are pertinent; however, as a general rule, debugging is outside the scope of this book.

Microsoft recommends that you enable Windows Installer logging before you install MCMS. This creates a log file to use for troubleshooting. If you've never run Windows Installer on your computer, you need to set up a key to enable Windows Installer logging. You must have local administrator rights.

Task 8-1. Enabling Windows Installer Logging

1. Launch the Registry Editor.

2. Navigate to HKEY_LOCAL_MACHINE\SOFTWARE\Policies\Microsoft\Windows\ Installer.

3. Add a key (string value) named Logging.

4. Give Logging the value voicewarmup.

5. Close the Registry Editor.

After logging is enabled, check your log file in the temp directory; your system recognizes %temp% as the path to the temporary directory.

Troubleshooting Installation and Configuration

Issues that you may encounter while you set up or upgrade generally pertain to missing platform requirements, Microsoft's patch management, SQL Server database access and compatibility, user accounts, or license problems with a particular MCMS edition.

Running the setup program is not covered in detail; however, Chapter 2 provides specific information about which MCMS components you should install on which computers.

If Setup Was Unsuccessful

The MCMS Installation Wizard attempts to detect required software components before it installs MCMS components. If the software is not detected, MCMS will not install a component dependent on the missing component. The wizard will stop and post an error message that installation was unsuccessful.

Task 8-2. Viewing Missing Software Requirements

1. Insert the MCMS CD in your CD-ROM drive, and then double-click setup.exe.

2. Click Install Components and then click Install MCMS Components.

3. On the License Agreement page, click I accept the terms in the license agreement, and then click Next.

   On the Custom Setup page, an X beside a component name indicates that a required application is missing and therefore the component will not be installed.

4. For every component with an X, select This feature Will Be Installed on Local Hard Drive from the drop-down list to the left of the component name, and then click Next.

5. Click Back to return to the Custom Setup page.

6. Click Cancel to exit the Installation Wizard.

■**Note** For additional information, refer to Microsoft's Installation Guide at `http://go.microsoft.com/fwlink/?LinkId=9918`.

Initialization Errors

If you observe unusually slow restarts on some computers, check the event log for the following messages:

```
Event Type: Error
Event Source: Service Control Manager
Event Category: None
Event ID: 7022
Description:
The Simple Mail Transport Protocol (SMTP) service hung on starting.
Event Type: Error
Event Source: Service Control Manager
Event Category: None
Event ID: 7022
Description:
The World Wide Web Publishing Service hung on starting.
```

Slow initialization of MCMS tracing during IIS initialization appears to the Service Control Manager as a hung service. Restart and let the initialization continue. Check the event log to verify that the services successfully start.

.NET Framework 1.1 Compatibility

If you load an ASP.NET application, and then receive the

```
A potentially dangerous Request.Form value was detected from
 the client
```

error message, you need to disable the request validation. .NET Framework 1.1 has a new attribute (`validateRequest`) that is not compatible with .NET Framework 1.0. This attribute is not compatible with ASP.NET 1.0. If you move your MCMS Web application `Web.config` files (or the MCMS 2002

Web.config files) to a computer running ASP.NET 1.0, then neither your MCMS Web application nor MCMS 2002 will work properly until this attribute is removed. If you target your MCMS Web application and MCMS 2002 to use .NET Framework 1.1, then the validateRequest attribute must be added (and set to false) in one of the following:

- All applications on your computer
- All MCMS Web sites (and in MCMS itself)

Note Refer to Knowledge Base article 821343 http://go.microsoft.com/ fwlink/?LinkId=18386.

Task 8-3. Setting Request Validation to False (for All Applications)

1. Browse to %Windir%\Microsoft.NET\Framework\v.1.1.xxxx\CONFIG\.

2. Launch Notepad, and then open the machine.config file.

3. Locate the Pages tag, and then set the validateRequest attribute to false as shown in the following:

```
<configuration>
<system.web>
<pages validateRequest="false" />
</system.web>
</configuration>
```

Task 8-4. Setting Request Validation to False for Your MCMS Web Applications

1. Launch Information Services Manager (in the Administrative Tools group), and then select Internet.

2. Expand Web Sites, expand Default Web, and then select your MCMS Web site.

3. Launch Notepad, and then open Web.config.

4. Locate the Pages tag, and set the validateRequest attribute to false, as shown in the following:

```
<configuration>
<system.web>
<pages validateRequest="false" />
</system.web>
</configuration>
```

Task 8-5. Disabling Request Validation for All MCMS Internal Applications

1. Click Explore and then browse to `<installation directory>\Program Files\ Microsoft Content Management Server\Server\IIS_CMS\OfficeWizard`.

2. Launch Notepad and then open the `Web.config` file.

3. Locate the `Pages` tag; set the `validateRequest` attribute to `false` in the following code:

```
<configuration>
<system.web>
<pages validateRequest="false" />
</system.web>
</configuration>
```

4. Repeat these steps for the following files:

```
\Program Files\Microsoft Content Management Server\Server\MCMS
\Program Files\Microsoft Content Management Server\Server\
MCMS\MCMSHomeport
\Program Files\Microsoft Content Management Server\Server\
MCMS\sitedeployment
```

Microsoft also provides the following information:

- "Request Validation—Preventing Script Attacks" at `http://www.asp.net/ faq/RequestValidation.aspx#2`.

- "`<pages>` Element" at `http://msdn.microsoft.com/library/en-us/ cpgenref/html/gngrfpagessection.asp`.

- "Protecting Against Script Exploits in a Web Application" at `http://msdn. microsoft.com/library/en-us/vbcon/html/vbtskProtectingAgainst➥ ScriptExploitsInWebApplication.asp`.

Upgrading from MCMS 2000 to MCMS 2002

The following are known issues that may need a manual follow-up when you upgrade to MCMS 2002 with SP1a.

Video-Only Placeholder Controls

Video-only placeholders are not supported in MCMS 2002. The problem can be worked around when video-only placeholders in your templates are upgraded to single-attachment placeholders.

■**Note** Microsoft gives more information in the migration report located at `Program Files\Microsoft Content Management Server\LogFiles\MigrationReport.txt`.

Some Characters for Object Properties Are Not Supported in MCMS 2002

MCMS 2002 checks for invalid characters. If you receive an error message, the invalid characters must be removed before you can save the object.

■**Note** Microsoft gives more information on valid character sets in the MCMS .NET Class Reference that is available in the online product documentation.

Default Channel Rendering Script

New channels inherit channel rendering scripts from their parents. After you upgrade to MCMS 2002, you can edit channel properties in Site Manager to remove the `ScriptURL` entry.

Template Gallery Contents

If the Add and Remove buttons are disabled in the Collection Editor, you need to double-check permissions in the template gallery items. You need to log on as an administrator to change permissions. The Add and Remove buttons are enabled in the placeholder definition Collection Editor.

Rights to Directories Are Not Migrated

After migrating, modify permissions to explicitly grant the appropriate users permissions to the following directories:

- `Program Files\Microsoft Content Management Server\Server\exeres\templates`

- `Program Files\Microsoft Content Management Server\Server\exeres\Channel_rendering_scripts`

- `Program Files\Microsoft Content Management Server\Server\rdonyres\MigratedResources`

Uninstalling MCMS 2002

The following are known issues when you uninstall MCMS 2002 with SP1a.

Uninstalling MCMS 2002 (SP1a) on Windows Server 2003

Make sure you close Visual Studio .NET before you uninstall MCMS 2002 with SP1a. If Visual Studio .NET is running, you may receive the following error message:

```
Package Microsoft Content Management Server
has failed to load properly.
```

If you receive the error, reinstall MCMS 2002 with SP1a, close Visual Studio .NET, and uninstall again.

Update Files After Uninstall

Back up the following files before you uninstall MCMS 2002 (SP1a) and restore them when you have completed the uninstall:

- `Program Files\Microsoft Content Management Server\Server\exeres\templates`

- `Program Files\Microsoft Content Management Server\Server\exeres\Channel_rendering_scripts`

- `Program Files\Microsoft Content Management Server\Server\rdonyres\MigratedResources`

You must also grant read/write access to appropriate users. (Permissions will be removed during the upgrade.)

Flush the Client Browser Cache

MCMS site resources are cached by Internet Explorer. When you uninstall MCMS 2002 (SP1a), resources on servers revert back to a previous version, but Internet Explorer still contains 2002-based resources, potentially causing scripting errors.

Task 8-6. Emptying the Temporary Internet Folder

1. Launch Internet Explorer.

2. Click Tools ➤ Internet Options.

3. Click Delete Files in the Temporary Internet Files section of the General tab.

4. Verify the deletion, and then close Internet Explorer.

Cannot Reinstall MCMS After Uninstalling MCMS 2002

If you get error 1607: "Unable to install the InstallShield Scripting Runtime," then check the following:

- Add/Remove Programs contains no MCMS entries.

- MCMS installation directory contains user-created files only.

- The Registry key `HKLM\Software\NCompass` directory contains no MCMS Registry entries.

If any remnants remain, you need to remove certain files and entries completely and rerun the MCMS Installation Wizard.

Task 8-7. Completing Removal

1. Remove any MCMS entries from the currently installed list in Add/Remove Programs.

2. Delete any files that are not customized files from the MCMS installation directory.

3. Delete any MCMS Registry entries in the `HKLM\Software\NCompass` directory.

MCMS 2002 Standard Edition

The following are known issues associated with uninstalling MCMS 2002 (SP1a), Standard Edition.

Membership in Roles

Standard Edition membership limits roles other than subscriber in the following ways:

- Allows 15 users who do not belong to the subscriber role to log on to the server.
- Adds Active Directory groups only to subscribers.

  If more than 15 users who are not subscribers are logged on, then

- Only an administrator can log on.
- The error is entered in the event log.

Standard Edition Limits Cluster Support

Members of the subscriber role can only log on to the named server in a cluster. Members of the author role can only log on to the authoring server (and are denied access to the named server). In a clustered development environment on servers other than the named server, developers who are *not* members of the subscriber role can access the following:

- Visual Studio .NET
- Local Windows client
- Remote Windows client

  Developers who *are* members of the subscriber role can also access the following:

- Local Web client
- Remote Web client

  In a clustered production environment on the named server, users who are *not* members of the subscriber role can access the following:

- Visual Studio .NET
- Local client
- Remote client

  Users who *are* members of the subscriber role can access the following:

- Local Web client
- Remote Web client

Site Stager Support

Standard Edition does not support Site Stager.

Host Headers Support

Standard Edition does not support HTTP host header mapping. Microsoft recommends that you use Enterprise Edition to serve multiple domains by mapping channels to host header names. Users view channels by name (qualified domain names are not required). In the Standard Edition, the channel name is required for the entire domain computer.

SQL Server Database Issues

The following are known issues with the SQL database when you upgrade.

Do Not Use sa Login for SQL Server

Using sa as the SQL Server login, especially with the No Password option, is a known security risk. Microsoft recommends that you change the SQL Server administrator login account to include the password.

No Upgrade for Different Language Versions

Make sure you upgrade to the same language you used from the original version. To upgrade, MCMS 2002 moves data into a new database. If the original is in a different language from the upgrade instance, the upgrade will fail.

Restored MCMS 2001 Database

If you restored a backed-up MCMS 2001 database to an MCMS 2002 database during upgrade to MCMS 2002, the DCA will not detect or upgrade it. You need to run the DCA manually.

Moving Domains

User accounts are not changed when you move to a new domain. You need to create the DCA MCMS system account on the current domain, so you can configure the database. Delete the existing MCMS system account.

MCMS System Account Errors

MCMS requires a database access account. Administrative privileges must be granted to SQL Server before you can configure the MCMS database using the DCA. You can use the MCMS system account or specify another valid SQL Server user account. If you use the MCMS system account as the database account, account validation errors may occur. If you want to avoid error messages saying that account passwords have expired, set the Password Never Expires option.

Task 8-8. Creating a Database

1. Launch Enterprise Manager in SQL Server.

2. Expand the Console Root and browse Databases.

3. Click Databases ➤ New Database.

4. Type the name of a database in the New Database dialog box.

5. Save changes.

Note Database naming conventions cannot contain numbers alone, but can contain a mixture of letters and numbers, and the underscore "_" character. Do not use a Transact-SQL reserved word in the database name. SQL Server reserves both the uppercase and lowercase versions of reserved words.

Task 8-9. Granting MCMS System Account Rights

1. Launch Enterprise Manager in SQL Server.

2. Expand the Microsoft SQL Servers node, and navigate to the MCMS database server.

3. Expand the Security node, click Logins, and then click New Login.

4. Click Browse in the New Login dialog box to locate the system account user.

5. Select a local computer (or domain) belonging to system account user in List Names From.

6. Add the system account user in Names, and then save changes.

7. Select the system account user in the Logins pane; click to view Properties.

8. In the SQL Server Login Properties dialog box, select the MCMS database from the Database Access tab in the Permit pane. Roles appear in Permit in Database Role.

9. Select db_ddladmin, db_datareader, and db_datawriter in the Permit in Database Role pane, and save the changes.

10. Exit the Enterprise Manager.

MCMS 2000 (SP3) Database User

The DCA and the SCA may not recognize a database user and its database rights.

■Note For additional information, refer to Knowledge Base article 305711 at `http://go.microsoft.com/fwlink/?LinkId=18411`.

You must define the MCMS system account and add the database user to the MCMS system database role.

Task 8-10. Defining the MCMS System Account

1. Launch Enterprise Manager in SQL Server.
2. Expand the SQL Servers node, and locate the MCMS database server.
3. Expand the Security node, select Logins, and then select New Login.
4. Add the MCMS system account or add a new SQL Login.
5. Select the MCMS database, and then add this user.
6. Select permissions `ddladmin`, `db_datareader`, and `db_datawriter`.
7. Save changes.

Task 8-11. Adding Database Users to the MCMS System Database Role

1. Launch the Enterprise Manager.
2. Locate the MCMS database, expand Databases, and then expand the MCMS database.
3. Select the Roles icon to display database roles.
4. Add the MCMS system account.

You must add this user to this database before you attempt to add it to a database role.

Windows Server 2003 and MCMS 2002

The following are known issues with MCMS 2002 (SP1a) on Windows Server 2003 when you upgrade.

Installing Visual Studio .NET 2002 on Windows Server 2003

If you receive the "Unable to pre-create directory for profile files" error message, refer to Knowledge Base article 320930 at `http://go.microsoft.com/fwlink/?LinkID=18359`.

MCMS Default Console

Add the MCMS Web site to the Trusted Sites in Internet Explorer. The MCMS default console may not work because the Internet zone High Security Level setting prevents the Switch to Edit Site JavaScript file download.

Task 8-12. Adding an MCMS Web Site to Trusted Sites

1. Use Internet Explorer to browse to the site that you want to add.
2. Click Add This Site To, and then select Trusted Sites Zone.
3. Click Add in the Trusted Sites dialog box.
4. Refresh from the new zone.
5. Confirm that the site is in the Trusted Sites Zone.

AESecurityService Restart

If you manually stop AESecurityService and attempt to access the MCMS Web site, the AESecurityService may not automatically restart. This leaves the MCMS Web site unavailable. Restart AESecurityService manually.

Task 8-13. Manually Restarting AESecurityService

1. In the Control Panel, launch Administrative Tools, and then Services.
2. Start AESecurityService.

Cannot Create Visual Studio .NET 2002 Web Application

If you are unable to create a Web application using Visual Studio .NET 2002 (running on IIS 6 on Windows Server 2003), it is because of mismatched file types.

■Note For additional information, refer to Knowledge Base article 327283 at http://go.microsoft.com/fwlink/?LinkId=18383.

Site Deployment in Windows Server 2003

If you receive The remote server returned an error: (404) Not Found error message, the ASP.NET user has not been granted permission to access the site deployment directory on Windows Server 2003.

Task 8-14. Granting Access to ASP.NET Users

1. Browse to inetpub\.

2. Select the wwwroot folder. Right-click on the folder and then click Properties.

3. In the wwwroot Properties dialog box, select the Security tab and click Add.

4. Select Locations and then Local Computer in the Select Users or Groups dialog box. Verify the selection.

5. In the text box, enter **aspnet**, and click Check Names.

6. Verify the changes.

7. The ASP.NET account has the following permissions in the Permissions for ASP.NET Machine Account:

   • Read and Execute

   • List Folder Contents

   • Read

8. Save changes.

Site Deployment Import on Windows Server 2003

The error message

```
An underlying connection was closed. An unexpected error
  occurred.
```

while importing data means that the IIS timed out. Modify the connection time in IIS.

Task 8-15. Modifying IIS Timeout Connection

1. Launch Internet Information Services Manager.

2. Expand Web Sites, and view Properties for the Default Web Site.

3. In the Web Site tab, increase the Connection Timeout to accommodate the import.

4. Save changes.

Using MCMS Administration Tools

The following are known issues you might encounter when using MCMS administrative tools.

Site Manager

MCMS 2002 Site Manager allows you to manage site architecture, but it's not a content authoring tool. You need administrative access to use it.

Modify Members Dialog Box

If new accounts have been added (on the domain), but do not appear in the Modify Members dialog box, you can force a refresh by selecting Synchronize. If the accounts are still not listed, manually enter them. If an error message is posted while you are trying to manually enter users and groups, the MCMS server is not configured correctly.

Task 8-16. Configuring the MCMS Server

1. Launch the SCA.

2. Select the Access tab and then click Configure.

3. Enter the name of the MCMS server and add it to supported NT domains.

4. Save changes and close the SCA.

Container Assignments

Any changes you make while you edit the rights group are live. An alternative way to assign channel access is to modify channel properties.

Task 8-17. Changing Rights Group Access

1. Launch Site Manager.

2. Select the Channels icon to display the channels hierarchy.

3. Expand Channels, locate and right-click the channel on which you want to change rights group membership, and then click Properties.

4. Select the Rights tab and click Modify.

5. In the User Rights page:

- Select the rights group container, and then the rights group to which you want to assign channel access.

- Add the rights group to the channel or click Add Parent's Right. (To view channel pages, a user must have rights to parent channels in the channel hierarchy.)

6. Save changes and close the Site Manager.

Hidden and Important Flags

MCMS Site Manager does not provide a visual indicator when the Important property is set to `true` for channels and pages. Additionally, there is no visual indication when the Hide When Published property is set to `true` for a page. A change in the appearance of a channel icon indicates that the Hide When Published property is set to `true` for that channel. Setting the Important flag does not affect an MCMS site unless a developer uses it in the design of the site.

You can view and modify the values of the following properties through the MCMS Publishing API:

- ChannelItem.IsHiddenModePublished
- Channel.IsImportant
- Posting.IsHiddenModePublished
- Posting.IsImportant

Specialized Language Fonts

You must set both the Locale and the Default Language to the appropriate region and font. This includes the Display Name for multilingual channels. Use one of the following methods to use channels and pages that require different language scripts managed on the same MCMS 2002 server:

- Install Site Manager on individual computers, one each for each language with the appropriate Locale and Default Language settings, and use those computers to manage the channels that require special fonts.

- Before accessing channel properties that require special fonts, switch the Locale and Default Language settings on the Site Manager computer to the appropriate language for the channel.

Active Directory Group Members Cannot Log On

If an Active Directory group is not configured as a security group (rather than as a distribution group), members may appear in MCMS rights groups but are not able to log on to the MCMS using Web Author or Site Manager. Create Active Directory *security groups* to grant rights. Security groups can be referenced in ACLs or used as e-mail aliases. Distribution groups are not security enabled.

Site Stager

Before you use MCMS Site Stager, you must install Site Stager on the source server and grant access to the remote staging computers.

Site Stager works with ASP-based sites only.

Staging Fails and No Event Is Reported

If you want Site Stager to run as a Windows scheduled task, you must configure the staging profile and the scheduling feature. Install the Site Stager scheduling feature, and then create a scheduled task that runs the staging profile automatically.

Task 8-18. Creating a Staging Profile

1. Launch the Site Stager, and log on as the site manager.

2. Click Start.

3. Click Add in the Site Stager Administration dialog box.

4. In the Properties dialog box, edit the following:

   • Type a name for the staging profile.

   • Select Active to enable automatic scheduling.

   • Type the `<domain>\<user name>` for the Stage-As user account.

   • Select Users group in the Modify Members–Stage-As dialog box, and then select Members.

   • Type a password.

   • Type the name of the file to be used as the default, top-level page for the staged site.

   • In the Browse for Folder dialog box, select the destination directory, and then click OK.

   • Select Shell After Staging to type the path of the program to be run after staging is complete.

   • Type a description for the staging profile.

5. Save changes and exit the Site Stager.

After you have configured the staging profile, you may schedule automated staging.

Task 8-19. Scheduling Automated Staging

1. Launch the Site Stager and log on as the site manager.

2. In the Site Stager Administration dialog box, double-click the staging profile you want to schedule.

3. On the Schedule tab of the Properties dialog box, do the following:

   • Select a staging interval.

   • Enter the start time for the staging.

   • Set the appropriate schedule information for the interval you have selected.

4. Click Apply, verify the scheduler, and then exit the Site Stager.

Note Interval options include
- Daily
- Weekly
- Monthly
- Once
- At System Startup
- At Logon
- When idle

The profile must be marked active to be staged automatically. Only one profile may be staged at a time to a destination directory.

Note If you are staging more than one profile to a *destination directory* using the automated scheduler, you must ensure they cannot run concurrently. You must also ensure that there is enough unused space to accommodate both sets of staged pages.

LDAP User Cannot Use the Site Stager

Do not use LDAP user accounts with Site Stager. An LDAP user is not allowed to stage a site. A Windows user account is required. Refer to Chapter 7.

Site Stager Status Does Not Refresh

The Site Stager status will not refresh if the profile's Properties dialog box is opened during the staging process. Close the Properties dialog box to allow Site Stager to refresh.

Staging Profiles Sharing the Same Destination Directory

An error will occur if two staging profiles try to stage the same destination directory concurrently. It is best not to have multiple profiles staging the same destination. However, if two profiles must share the same destination directory, you must ensure the first staging results are moved out of the destination directory before the next staging occurs. Because subsequent staging results will overwrite existing files, it is prudent to check the unused space on the drive containing the destination directory before the staging begins.

Profile Fails to Stage

A valid profile stages automatically according to the schedule you set for it. If a profile fails to stage, verify that

- The profile has a unique name.
- It contains the correct directory of the site to be staged.
- Channels to be staged exist.
- A schedule has been set to stage at the staging frequency you expect.
- The program you want to launch after staging is identified by its complete path and the arguments are separated by spaces.

Supporting Authors

The following known problems may be encountered when using MCMS site authoring tools (Authoring Connector and Web Author).

Authoring Connector Missing or Unavailable from the File Menu in Word

The Authoring Connector should be available on the File menu in Word. If it's missing or unavailable, the Authoring Connector add-in may not have been registered or there was a background instance of Word running during installation. You must verify if the installation was a success, and allow the add-in by accepting any warning dialog boxes. You must close all instances of Word before you reinstall it.

Empty Task List (Authoring Connector Wizard)

An Authoring Connector task list will appear to be empty if a user does not have rights to the channels and templates referenced by tasks in the list or if the list is not stored in the correct location. To display the Authoring Connector Wizard task list, you must ensure that

- The user has rights to the referenced templates and channels.
- The XML file (Publishing Tasks.xml) is valid—some characters will cause an XML file to be invalid.
- The path for channels and templates is correct ($CMSroot\server\ IIS_CMS\OfficeWizard\). You can change the default location in Web.config for Authoring Connector.

Connected Page Changes Do Not Appear

If connected pages are not viewable in MCMS Authoring Connector after changes have been made, do the following:

- Check each page using Preview Connected Pages.
- Make sure the user has at least subscriber rights for template galleries.
- Use Go to Connected Page to view a list of pages connected to the current one; use Go To for viewing pages.

Connected Pages Fail to Expire

Connected pages expire on independent schedules other than the original schedule. Change the expiration date of connected pages to the same day or manually delete orphaned pages that have not expired. Editors, moderators, template designers, and channel managers can delete pages in channels for which they have rights. Authors can delete public pages or pages they own.

Task 8-20. Deleting and Restoring Pages

1. Launch Site Manager, and log on as channel manager.
2. Click the Channel icon to display the channel hierarchy.
3. Select the channel that contains the page you want to delete, and then select the items.
4. Click Delete to move items to the Deleted Items container.
5. To restore the page, move it from the Deleted Items container back into the channel hierarchy.

Removing a page deletes it permanently from the system. A page must be deleted before it can be permanently removed.

Task 8-21. Removing Pages

1. Launch Site Manager, and log on as channel manager.
2. Click the Channels icon to display the channel hierarchy.
3. Expand Deleted Items, and then click Delete to remove the page.

Page Approval Does Not Match Author and Editor Rights

If a writer updates content that is used on multiple connected pages while the editor approves the content for one page, the content is approved for all pages, regardless of author or editor rights.

Cannot Modify Custom Properties

You must be an administrator, a channel manager, or a template designer to modify custom properties.

Internet Explorer Fails on Placeholder

Internet Explorer 5.5 with SP1 or SP2 fails when you author HTML placeholder controls. You must upgrade to Internet Explorer 6.0.

Attachment Image Error

In Web Author, a new Resource Manager may find file attachments that have been uploaded are broken the first time they are inserted. Reinsert the attachment.

Cannot Refresh Approval Assistant

Close and restart the Approval Assistant when it does not refresh.

Multiple Placeholders Bound to the Same Definition

The HTML placeholder definition. `PlaceholderToBind` property, must have a one-to-one relationship with HTML, single-image, and single-attachment placeholder controls. Visual Studio does not enforce this relationship. If you bind more than one placeholder to the same definition, you may observe unexpected runtime behavior.

Dealing with Visual Studio .NET Issues

Visual Studio .NET is the primary tool for developing MCMS Web applications. Visual Studio is based on the Microsoft .NET Framework. To deploy an MCMS Web application, the target computers must have .NET Framework for the applications to run.

Visual Studio 2002 installs .NET Framework 1.0 as part of its environment. Visual Studio 2003 installs .NET Framework 1.1. There are compatibility issues as noted in the following subsections.

■**Note** Windows Server 2003 requires .NET Framework 1.1 (.NET Framework 1.0 is not supported).

MCMS 2002 (SP1a) with Visual Studio .NET

Visual Studio .NET 2002 is based on .NET Framework 1.0. Target computers must have a .NET Framework installed for these applications to run. If the target computers are running Windows Server 2003, you must upgrade .NET Framework 1.0 to .NET Framework 1.1.

Note   Refer to the product documentation section "Using MCMS 2002 with SP1a with .NET Framework 1.1" for additional information.

New ASP.NET Application

Restart SQL Server before creating a new MCMS ASP.NET application.

If SQL Server is stopped, creating a new MCMS ASP.NET-based application will take a long time to complete. You may also reduce the "new application" time by modifying the ODBC (Online Database Connectivity) timeout (Microsoft recommends 30 seconds).

If you are unsure about what is happening, view the application log and look for the message:

```
SQL Server does not exist or access denied.
```

This message is indicative of the issue.

Placeholder-Template Anomalies

A grid layout for design of a template may cause placeholder controls to appear in unexpected locations (controls may even overlap, hiding the bottom control).Use a table in FlowLayout for finer control of placeholder placement.

Errors Binding Placeholder Controls to Definitions

If you are unable to bind a placeholder control to the placeholder definition, the PlaceholderToBind property may not be set correctly.

To bind the placeholder controls in a template file to their corresponding placeholder definitions in the associated template, you must set the PlaceholderToBind property correctly.

Task 8-22. Setting the `PlaceholderToBind` Property

1. Select the control in the Visual Studio .NET template file.

2. Select `PlaceholderToBind` in the Properties window.

3. From the drop-down list of `PlaceholderToBind`, select the appropriate placeholder definition.

Note If the `PlaceholderToBind` value is set to `none` or the drop-down list is missing the `PlaceholderDefinition` names, you must ensure that the ASP.NET file is correctly bound to the Template Gallery Item and the missing `PlaceholderDefinition` is of a type supported by the selected `PlaceholderControl`.

Cannot View Select File Dialog Box

An invalid virtual directory to the Web Project will cause the Select File dialog box not to be viewable.

Task 8-23. Configuring the Virtual Directory

1. Launch the IIS Metabase editor, and navigate to the virtual directory for the Web project.

2. Set the value of the `KeyType` property (ID 1002) to the string `IIsWebVirtualDir`. If it doesn't exist, you must create it using these values:

   - User Type = `Server`
   - Data Type = `String`
   - Data = `IIsWebVirtualDir`

Task 8-24. Selecting a Template from the Select File Dialog Box

1. Launch Visual Studio .NET.

2. Open Template Explorer and select the template you want to edit.

3. Open the Select File dialog box and edit properties.

4. Use the tree control to locate the virtual directory that contains the template.

5. Select the template from the list.

6. Choose Select.

7. Edit and save changes to the template.

Cannot Load Root Template Gallery

If the error message

```
Cannot load root template gallery
```

appears when trying to access the root Template Gallery and you are not able to access Template Explorer, you must check the user credentials to the root template gallery and then refresh Visual Studio .NET. If the problem persists, restart Visual Studio .NET. If it still persists, reinstall Visual Studio .NET.

MCMS Options Do Not Appear in Visual Studio .NET

If the Enable as MCMS Project option is not available (Visual Studio .NET), you must regenerate DeveloperTools.xml as a valid XML file.

Task 8-25. Regenerating DeveloperTools.xml

1. Close Visual Studio .NET.

2. Delete all files in \Documents and Settings\<User>\Application Data\ Microsoft\Visual Studio\7.0\.

3. Restart Visual Studio .NET.

The deleted files will be re-created.

Cannot Browse IIS Web Sites Located on Localhost

Visual Studio .NET–MCMS applications only allow access to the default MCMS-IIS Web site (on port 80). To change the port, manually configure the port.

Task 8-26. Configuring Visual Studio .NET-MCMS Integration

1. Launch Notepad, and open `DeveloperTools.xml` located in `Program Files\ Microsoft Content Management Server\DevTools\DeveloperTools.xml`.

2. Locate these statements:

```
<CmsEnvironment>
    <Server BaseUrl="http://localhost" InstanceId="1"/>
</CmsEnvironment>
```

3. Use the `InstanceID` property to access a different site.

4. Save changes, and exit Notepad.

■**Note** Use the Metabase Editor (MetaEdit) to determine the instance ID of an IIS Web site (`LM\W3SVC\<instance ID>`).

XML Placeholder Timeout Error

If `The operation has timed-out` error message appears while setting XML placeholder contents, use a file reference for local `.xsd` files instead of an HTTP-based URL. Microsoft IIS has trouble resolving HTTP-based URLs to the local computer (for example, URL `http://localhost/file.xsd`).

Summary

In this chapter, we covered troubleshooting issues related to setting up, upgrading, configuring, and uninstalling MCMS. We discussed issues related to the operation of administration tools (Site Manager and Site Stager). Finally, we covered integrating CMS with Visual Studio.

Additional Resources

The following list of troubleshooting resources appears in the MCMS documentation:

- Debugging topics
- Microsoft Visual Studio .NET Help
- Microsoft SQL Server Help

- Microsoft SharePoint Server Integration Pack Help
- Microsoft Content Management Server 2002 Readme
- Microsoft Content Management Server 2002 Installation CD
- Microsoft Content Management Server Web site. `http://www.microsoft.com/cmserver/`

    TechNet resources include

- Technical articles and tools for planning, development, and deployment.
- Products & Technology page. `http://go.microsoft.com/fwlink/?LinkId=5160`
- MSDN information
- Integrated server software, technical documentation, and white papers. `http://go.microsoft.com/fwlink/?LinkId=5161`
- Microsoft Servers site
- Products for IT professionals and developers. `http://go.microsoft.com/fwlink/?LinkId=6732`
- Newsgroups
    - Microsoft newsgroups. `http://go.microsoft.com/fwlink/?LinkId=9960`
- Premier Support

    Access to specialized technical expertise, geared at enterprises:

- Microsoft Premier Support for Enterprise Systems
- Microsoft Premier Support for Developers
- Microsoft Premier Support for MCSPs
- Microsoft Premier Support for Original Equipment Manufacturers (OEMs)
- Microsoft Authorized Premier Support

PART 3

Templates

CHAPTER 9

MCMS Development Using Page Objects

This chapter covers

- Processing pages
- Examining an MCMS application
  - Visual Studio and MCMS
  - MCMS .NET class reference
  - MCMS COM object reference
- Developing templates
  - Template development procedures
  - MCMS Author Connector templates
  - Creating MCMS publishing tasks
- Using the Web Author
  - Creating pages
  - Publishing pages
  - Updating pages
  - The MCMS Authoring Connector

This chapter explains the procedures for implementing MCMS objects, primarily templates and placeholders. This chapter does not show you how to code a Web application. We will cover MCMS-Visual Studio integration and the critical procedures for creating an MCMS solution, but we won't cover language specifics or code constructs. Many of the development procedures discussed in this chapter do involve writing PAPI and ASPX code to accomplish the specific goals of your site. Although we do not cover how to write this code, we do indicate what functional pieces are required where.

The big picture here is that MCMS is a rich environment for developing practical and efficient business Web solutions. The power, however, is not in the box—to get a cool portal app, you have to code it.

Processing Pages

The structure of this book to this point has been no frills or tangential side trips into MCMS concepts. Although we won't break our mold here, we will expand our discussion to include page processing.

What we know so far is that what MCMS serves up may look like a Web page to a browser, but it's actually a *posting*—a dynamic construct based on ASP template code, data from a database (and file system resources), all wrapped together with an MCMS-specific console.

Figure 9-1 traces the process of responding to page requests. We'll use this to see where you need to provide your customized code. MCMS responds to page requests by assembling postings. The way postings are rendered depends on the mode in which the browser is operating, *author* or *subscriber*. Content on pages looks different under each of these modes. Let's examine *presentation mode* first.

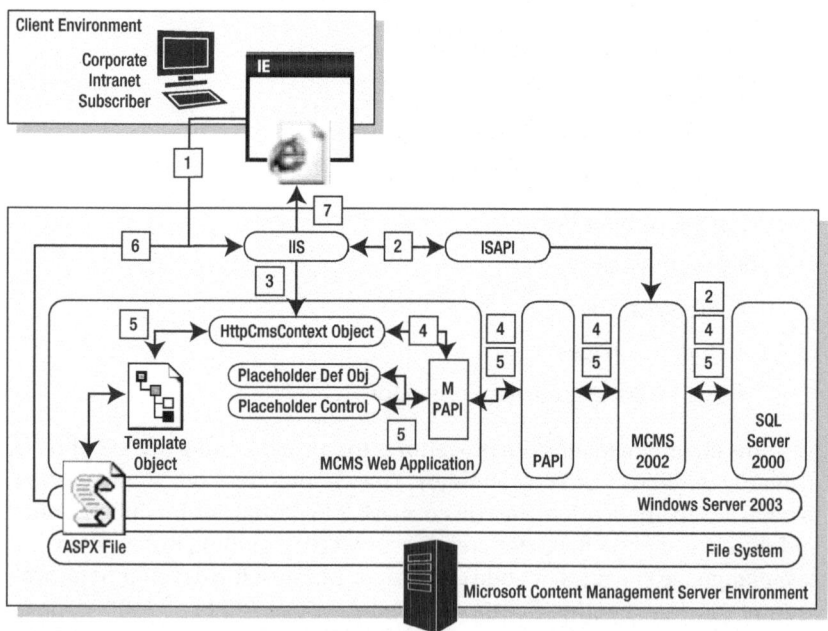

Figure 9-1. *How MCMS serves page requests*

The processes in Figure 9-1 are

1. The user clicks on a link to a page on the CMS site. Nothing looks or feels any different between the CMS site and any other Web site.

2. IIS (CMS-enabled) accepts and processes the page request. The page request is routed to the ISAPI filter (`ReAuthFilt.dll`), which splits the URL into the corresponding posting and template file and generates a new URL using the ASPX template file. The new URL contains unique query string parameters, including a GUID for the posting.

3. IIS passes the generated URL to `ASP.NET.DLL` and MCMS, which instantiates a `CmsHttpContext` object in which the ASPX template file is executed. A `Posting` object is initialized, a template object is initialized, and template data are extracted from the Content Repository.

4. Template files contain one or more placeholder controls. Placeholder data (content) are read from the Content Repository. The `PlaceholderDefinition` objects are instantiated from the Content Repository. These objects contain configuration and constraint information about controls.

5. During ASPX template execution, the `CmsHttpContext` object renders the placeholder controls, HTML, script, and other controls as a stream of HTML.

6. MCMS exposes a fairly straightforward page-processing object model (see Figure 9-2). The root object is the `CmsHttpContext` object. Contained within the context are `Channel` and `Posting` objects. Channels provide the logical structure of the MCMS site and postings are the "pages." A posting is assembled from a `Template` object, which contains placeholders for content. For a placeholder to be embedded into a template, a `Placeholder Definition` object must be associated with the `Template` object. A `Template` object is associated with a template file containing ASP code. Figure 9-2 illustrates the CMS object model. This object hierarchy is covered in the procedures delineated in the second half of the chapter. MCMS also manages a cache to expedite files that are used often.

Note The original URL identifies the location of the posting.

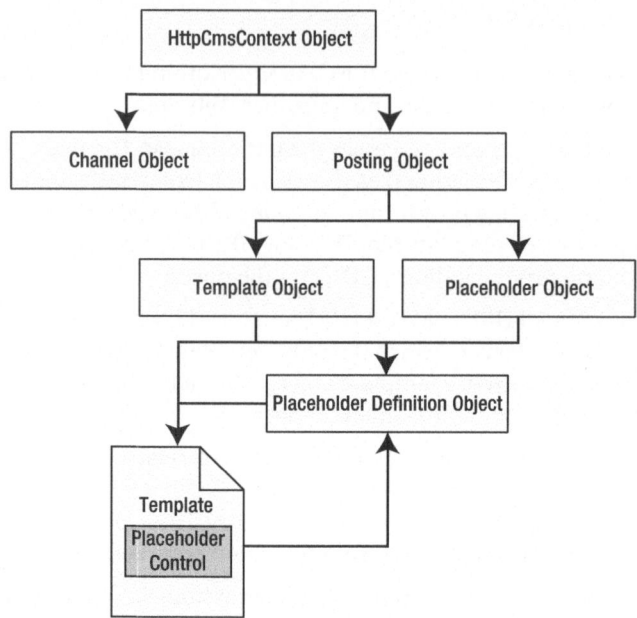

Figure 9-2. *CMS object model*

Examining an MCMS Application

As mentioned previously, an MCMS Web site is not just a collection of HTML documents; it's a dynamic application whose purpose is to make sense out of a lot of rapidly changing business information. Not only is it an application with input, storage, processing, and output functions, but it's also a distributed application with components potentially located in many different geographical areas.

MCMS is also a toolbox—a box of Legos—with which to build your distributed application. MCMS is also designed to fit seamlessly into a big, automated workshop: Visual Studio. In this chapter, we'll cover how to make these tools work in the MCMS context.

Visual Studio and MCMS

One of the significant areas of evolution in MCMS 2002 is direct integration with Visual Studio. Although support for building Web projects is not new in Visual Studio, MCMS is not a typical Web project. It has its own structure and components that Visual Studio manages for you. To develop solutions under MCMS, your development environment requires the following:

- Visual Studio 2003 (including the .NET Framework 1.1)
- MCMS 2002
- IIS
- MCMS Site Manager

■**Note** You'll need access SQL Server, but it does not have to be running on your local development machine.

MCMS makes different types of project templates available through the Visual Studio .NET IDE (find them by using the New Project dialog box). Two languages are supported: Visual Basic and Visual C#. Three types of projects are supported: Web application, Web service, and an empty Web project (see Table 9-1).

Table 9-1. *Visual Studio MCMS Project Types*

MCMS Web application	Application with a Web UI
MCMS Web service	XML-based Web service that can be used from other applications
MCMS empty Web project	Empty project

■**Note** A Visual Studio .NET "solution" is a container for one or more "projects." Solution settings are global among the child projects. For additional information, refer to the Visual Studio .NET Help.

Although similar to an ASP.NET-based project, an MCMS project differs in the following ways:

- References to MCMS components are added. (Do not remove default references.)
- The default console is added.
- An MCMS virtual directory is added to the project.
- An MCMS-specific Web.config file is added with MCMS HTTP modules.
- Web.config is updated with references to MCMS components.
- Tools such as the Template Explorer are made available within Visual Studio .NET.

Although you create an MCMS project using the New Project dialog box (see the next task), you are actually creating an MCMS *solution* that contains a project.

Task 9-1. Creating an MCMS Project

1. Launch Visual Studio.

2. Select File ➤ New Project.

3. In the New Project dialog box, expand the Content Management Server type.

4. Choose the language for your project: C# or VB .NET.

5. Choose the project type: Web Application, Web Service, or Empty Web Project.

6. Enter a name for your CMS application.

7. Browse to the location of the CMS site to set the location.

8. Identify whether or not the project is to be added to another project.

9. Select OK to build the application context with appropriate references and the default Web Authoring console.

When the new project has been spawned, examine the workspace. On the Tools menu, browse the tools listed under Content Management Server. These are the primary tools you installed in Chapter 2.

Note You can add another MCMS project to the solution by choosing File ➤ Add Project.

Task 9-2. Opening an MCMS Solution (Project)

1. Launch Visual Studio .NET.

2. Select File ➤ Open Solution.

3. Use the Open Solution dialog box to navigate to the solution file. Select the target file (`.sln`).

4. Select Open.

Task 9-3. Converting an ASP.NET Web Project into an MCMS Project

1. Launch Visual Studio .NET.

2. Open an existing ASP.NET Web solution (project).

3. Select Project ➤ Enable as MCMS Project. Two MCMS-specific windows are available:

   • The Content Management Server tab in the Toolbox window contains placeholder controls for use in template files.

■**Note** The Content Management Server tab is active only when an ASPX file is loaded in the editing window.

   • MCMS Template Explorer provides access to the template hierarchy. For convenience, you may dock it next to the Visual Studio .NET Solution Explorer.

■**Note** You must be an MCMS administrator, channel manager, or template developer to view the template hierarchy.

Task 9-4. Opening the Template Explorer

1. Launch Visual Studio.

2. Select File ➤ New Project.

3. Choose View ➤ Other Windows ➤ Template Explorer.

4. Dock the Template Explorer on the right side of the VS workspace (next to the Solution Explorer and Class Viewer).

Templates are dual objects: the logical Template Gallery item shown in the Template Explorer and the ASPX file containing the template code. In the second half of this chapter, we cover creating the logical objects and associating them with the code files.

MCMS .NET Class Reference

MCMS 2002 provides a rich .NET managed code environment to develop MCMS solutions:

- **Publishing**: Classes that constitute the core of the MCMS 2002 Publishing API (`Microsoft.ContentManagement.Publishing.dll`).

- **Publishing.Events**: Classes used for working with the event model (enables automated workflow) (`Microsoft.ContentManagement.Publishing.dll`).

- **Publishing.Extensions.Placeholders**: Classes used to implement placeholders; unique classes for different types of content (`Microsoft.ContentManagement.Publishing.Extensions.Placeholders.dll`).

- **Publishing.Extensions.Placeholders.Office**: Classes used to implement Authoring Connector placeholders; enables HTML and attachments to be authored in Word (`Microsoft.ContentManagement.Publishing.Extensions.Placeholders.Office.dll`).

- **Web**: ASP.NET Web application classes, includes `CmsHttpApplication` (`Microsoft.ContentManagement.Web.dll`).

- **Web.Caching**: Classes used for caching (`Microsoft.ContentManagement.Web.dll`).

- **Web.Security**: Classes for authentication (`Microsoft.ContentManagement.Web.dll`).

- **WebControls**: Classes have been updated for managed code compatibility (`Microsoft.ContentManagement.Publishing.dll`).

MCMS COM Object Reference

MCMS 2002 provides COM-based APIs: the enhanced (2002 version) publishing API and the site deployment API.

▪**Note** Use the .NET-based, managed code version of the publishing API for development. Refer to the .NET-based APIs in the MCMS .NET Class Reference.

Developing Templates

A template is an object that binds code, data, and resources, which are rendered as HTML to serve HTTP page requests. When you use Visual Studio for

MCMS solution development, you build templates into the Web solution, so authoring and display integrate seamlessly.

MCMS is template-driven, exclusively. To MCMS, a template is a template is a template. There is no functional difference among templates. Looking past the technology, however, portals are built to solve business information problems. Because of this, templates may, in fact, differ significantly in how they gather or present content. Further, the template used to gather information may not be the template used to present it. Take the training world, for example. *Sharable Content Objects* (the SCORM initiative) are generated by authors to an exacting specification, so they can be harvested by learners in very different contexts—same information, different templates. To inspire your thinking along these lines, we've created a simple template taxonomy based on functional position in an informational hierarchy. This taxonomy may not be appropriate for your application, but it's worth considering how templates structure information.

- **Leaf template**: The leaf is the lowest level of the hierarchical navigation scheme. This fundamental unit of information serves as its own information source. It may contain external links to ancillary information; however, it provides the details of the story with no—or at least minimal—scrolling. Good Web page design suggests that Web pages chunk information into screens. A good leaf template enforces this philosophy.

- **Aggregation template**: This template corresponds to a branch in a hierarchy. If there are multiple leaf pages relating to a single topic, some sort of integration is probably useful—even if it's just a listing of the leaf pages. Aggregation templates can provide summaries of associated details, integration of parts into a whole, or show some other quality such as the logical consequence of antecedent actions. Remember that what is being aggregated is dynamic, so aggregation templates must adjust semantically to changing leaves—you don't want to keep rewriting them.

- **Repurposing template**: This type of template is meant to take data acquired from another template (or set of templates) and repackage or repurpose those data. A simple type of repurposing template may be a printer-friendly reformatting of data. More often, repurposing is more complex. It may filter details to provide a synopsis. It may add explanatory information or integrate details from multiple sources. *Microsoft Content Management Server 2002, A Complete Guide* (Addison-Wesley Professional, 2003) offers a couple of useful guidelines: this type of template "is not meant to be used by content contributors," and it "reformats the content contained in pages created in a different but related template."

A last issue concerning template development may be relegated to technical training, but I doubt it. Templates are very important tools. In the MCMS context, they are more than important—they're essential. Templates, however, are meant to empower collaborative workers. When they are shoved down somebody's throat, they lose that warm, fuzzy, empowering feeling! Template design needs to be controlled, but it can't crystallize. Template development should be meta-stable—they can't change on a whim, but you do need to plan for template evolution. Create a way for content contributors to provide input about template design. Encouraging ownership will power up your empowerment strategy.

Template Development Procedures

Template objects must be created logically within the MCMS environment and implemented in code. Template objects are maintained in Template Galleries. Development procedures include creating the MCMS template object, coding a template file, and associating a template with the Web Authoring console. Implementing template placeholders to bind resources simplifies page creation and enforces consistency.

Note You must have administrator credentials or be a member of the developers group to create templates. You must also have read/write privileges to the containers to which you will be posting content.

Task 9-5. Creating a Template

1. Launch the Template Explorer, navigate to a template container, and select New Template. A new template named New Template appears in the template container.

2. Rename the new template (select Rename from the context menu).

3. Select File ➤ Save All to save your changes.

Your new template is now available in the MCMS Template Explorer under the gallery. The logical Template object has been created. Next an ASPX page to lay out boilerplate text, controls, placeholders, and scripts needs to be implemented and associated with Template objects.

Task 9-6. Creating a Template File

1. Launch the Solution Explorer.

2. Expand the target container, and select the `Templates` folder.

3. Select File ➤ Add New Item.

4. In the Add New Item window, select Content Management Server (Categories).

5. Select Template File from the Templates list.

6. Select Open.

The template file is now open for editing. A template file can be implemented using the default grid layout (absolute positioning) or flow layout.

Task 9-7. Laying Out a Template File

1. View the Properties window.

2. Select the `pageLayout` property in the Properties window.

3. Change the layout from GridLayout to FlowLayout.

4. Select HTML to display the HTML view.

5. Add HTML code to the `form` tag.

6. Select Save All to save your changes.

Task 9-8. Associating a Template File with a Template

1. Launch the Template Explorer, and select the new template.

2. Select `TemplateFile` from the Properties window, and click Browse (...) to display the File Open dialog box.

3. Navigate to the appropriate virtual directory, and click Select.

4. Select Save All to save changes.

Note The Template icon (Template Explorer) indicates an active association.

Placeholders provide a friendly, structured way for authors to add content. Different types of placeholder controls require different placeholder definitions to allow resource binding. Template designers manage the types of content by creating placeholder definitions with specific properties.

Task 9-9. Adding an HTML Placeholder Definition

1. Launch Template Explorer and select the new template.

2. View the Properties window.

3. Select `PlaceholderDefinitions` in the Properties window to open the Placeholder Definition Collection Editor.

4. Add an `HTMLPlaceholderDefinition`.

5. Set properties for the new placeholder definition:

   - **AllowHyperlinks**: True|False.

   - **AllowLineBreaks**: True|False.

   - **Formatting**: NoFormatting|FullFormatting.

   - **Description**: Enter a description for the template.

   - **Name**: Enter a title.

   - **AllowAttachments**: True|False.

   - **AllowImage**: True|False.

   - **MustUseResourceGallery**: True|False.

   - **UseGeneratedIcon**: True|False.

6. Save changes.

PLACEHOLDER DEFINITION PROPERTIES

Tables are derived from the MCMS, Site Development Product Documentation (`SiteDevl.chm`).

   `AllowLineBreaks` and `Formatting` properties determine what tags are allowed in an HTML placeholder control (see Table 9-2). Certain HTML tags cannot be used within an HTML placeholder control on a page. MCMS tag categories are shown in Table 9-3.

Table 9-2. `AllowLineBreaks` *and* `Formatting` *Properties*

Property Settings	Flow	List	Heading	Table	Markup	Font
`Formatting = FullFormatting` AND `AllowLineBreaks = True`	Yes	Yes	Yes	Yes	Yes	Yes
`Formatting = FullFormatting` AND `AllowLineBreaks = False`	Yes		Yes		Yes	Yes
`Formatting = HTMLStyles` AND `AllowLineBreaks = True`	Yes	Yes	Yes			
`Formatting = HTMLStyles` AND `AllowLineBreaks = False`	Yes		Yes			
`Formatting = TextMarkup` (regardless of `AllowLineBreaks` setting)					Yes	
`Formatting = TextMarkupAndHTML➥Styles` AND `AllowLineBreaks = True`	Yes	Yes	Yes		Yes	
`Formatting = TextMarkupAndHTML➥Styles` AND `AllowLineBreaks = False`	Yes		Yes		Yes	
`Formatting = NoFormatting` (regardless of `AllowLineBreaks` setting)						

Other tags (`<BR>`, `<A>`, and `<IMG>` handled with specific rules) are stripped out of content when it is entered into placeholders.

Continued

Table 9-3. *MCMS Tag Categories*

Tag Category	Tags in Category
Flow	<ADDRESS>, <BLOCKQUOTE>, <CENTER>, <DIV>, <HR>, <NOBR>, <PRE>, <Q>, <SPAN>, <WBR>
Heading	<DIR>, <H1>, <H2>, <H3>, <H4>, <H5>, <H6>, <MARQUEE>, <MENU>
List	<LI>, <OL>, <UL>
Table	<CAPTION>, <COL>, <COLGROUP>, <TABLE>, <TBODY>, <TD>, <TFOOT>, <TH>, <THEAD>, <TR>
Markup	<B>, <EM>, <I>, <STRONG>, <S>, <STRIKE>, <TT>, <ABBR>, <ACRONYM>, <CITE>, <CODE>, <DEL>, <DFN>, <INS>, <KBD>, <SAMP>, <VAR>, <BDO>, <RT>, <RUBY>, <BLINK>
Font	<FONT>

The <BR>, <A>, and <IMG> tags are also controlled by placeholder properties:

- AllowLineBreaks = True enables the <BR> tag (independent of AllowLineBreaks/Formatting in the preceding table).
- AllowHyperlinks = True enables the <A> tag.
- AllowImages = True enables the <IMG> tag.

Task 9-10. Adding Image Placeholder Definition

1. Launch Template Explorer and select the new template.
2. View the Properties window.
3. Select PlaceholderDefinitions in the Properties window to open the Placeholder Definition Collection Editor.
4. Add an ImagePlaceholderDefinition.
5. Set the properties of the new placeholder definition:
   - **AllowHyperlinks**: True|False.
   - **Description**: Enter a description.
   - **Name**: Enter a name.
   - **MustUseResourceGallery**: True|False.
6. Close the Placeholder Definition Collection Editor.
7. Select Save All to save your changes.

Placeholder controls provide a UI to support authoring and display. In live mode, a placeholder control renders an HTML stream; in author mode, it enables content to be edited.

Task 9-11. Adding an HTML Placeholder

1. Locate a template to edit using the Solution Explorer. Open in Design view (the Design and HTML are displayed at the lower edge of the window) and select Design.

2. View the Toolbox.

3. Select the Toolbox Content Management Server tab.

4. Place an `HTMLPlaceholderControl` on the template by dragging the control.

   The control's default name is `HtmlPlaceholderControl1`.

5. Select the placeholder control, and set the properties of the control:

   - **AllowHtmlSourceEditing**: True|False.
   - **EnableAuthoring**: True|False.
   - **EnableViewState**: True|False.
   - **ToolTip**: Enter a functional/operational description.
   - **Visible**: True|False.
   - **PlaceholderToBind**: Select Placeholder Definition.
   - **EditControlHeight**: Set control height.
   - **EditControlWidth**: Set control width.
   - **(ID)**: Enter a name.

6. Select Save All to save your changes.

Task 9-12. Adding a Single Image Placeholder

1. Locate a template to edit using the Solution Explorer. Open in Design view (the Design and HTML are displayed at the lower edge of the window, and select Design.

2. View the Toolbox.

3. Select the Toolbox Content Management Server tab.

4. Place a `SingleImagePlaceholderControl` on the template file.

   The control's default name is `SingleImagePlaceholderControl1`.

5. Select the placeholder control, and set its properties:

   - **EnableAuthoring**: Select True.
   - **EnableViewState**: Select True.

- **ToolTip**: Enter a functional/operational description.
- **Visible**: Select True.
- **PlaceholderToBind**: Select Placeholder Definition.
- **(ID)**: Type **AuthorPicture**.

6. Select Save All to save your changes.

Note   To drag and drop placeholder controls onto the template file, the template file must be in Design view.

Task 9-13. Adding an XML Placeholder

1. Locate a template to edit using the Solution Explorer. Open in Design view.

2. View the Toolbox.

3. Select the Toolbox Content Management Server tab.

4. Place an XMLPlaceholderControl on the template file.

5. Select the placeholder control, and set its properties:

   - **Description**: Default value is <none>; description of placeholder definition.

   - **ManageCmsUrls**: Default value is True; determines whether MCMS will detect and handle URLs of resources.

   - **Name**: Default value is NewXmlPlaceholderDefinition; identifies unique placeholder definition.

   - **Type**: Value is XmlPlaceholderDefinition type of the placeholder definition (read-only).

   - **CheckForValidity**: Default value is True; determines whether XML must be valid.

   - **CheckForWellFormedness**: Default value is True; determines whether XML must be well formed.

   - **XsdUrl**: Default value is <none>; if the CheckForValidity property is set to the default True, this property must be set to a valid URL for an appropriate XSD file.

6. Select Save All to save your changes.

The Web Author console (enables authoring from a browser) is bound to a Template Gallery (and code provided) from within a Visual Studio project.

Task 9-14. Adding the Web Author Console to a Template File

1. Open a template for editing using the Solution Explorer. Select Design view.

2. Expand the template container; expand Console in Solution Explorer.

3. Place the `DefaultConsole.ascx` control on the template.

4. Select Save All to save changes.

MCMS Authoring Connector Templates

The MCMS Authoring Connector enables Word 2002 to be used as the authoring tool. In many cases where MCMS is supporting large-scale information exchange, Word is the overwhelming tool of choice among authors. The Authoring Connector provides content editing and publishing capabilities using the familiar Word UI.

Development tasks include creating a template and a publishing task that is accessible and executed from within Word.

Identically to Web Author, you create an Authoring Connector template and template file, and then associate them.

Task 9-15. Creating an Authoring Connector Template

1. Open your project in Visual Studio .NET.

2. Navigate to or create the Template Gallery.

3. Open or create a template to edit

4. Open or create a template file.

5. Associate the template file with the template.

Note The procedures are identical for Authoring Connector templates and Web author templates. (Refer to Tasks 9-16 through 9-19.)

Similarly to Web Author procedures, placeholder definitions and placeholder controls are added to templates.

Task 9-16. Adding an Office HTML Placeholder Definition

1. Use the Template Explorer to select a template into which you add placeholder definitions.

2. Select the `Placeholder Definitions` property in the Properties window, and then open the Placeholder Definition Collection Editor.

3. Add an `OfficeHtmlPlaceholderDefinition`. A generic placeholder definition is displayed.

4. Use the Placeholder Definition Collection Editor to set properties of the placeholder definition:

   - **AllowHyperlinks**: True|False.

   - **AllowLineBreaks**: True|False.

   - **Formatting**: Select NoFormatting|FullFormatting.

   - **Description**: Enter a description.

   - **Name**: Enter a name.

   - **AllowAttachments**: True|False.

   - **AllowImage**: True|False.

   - **MustUseResourceGallery**: True|False.

   - **UseGeneratedIcon**: True|False.

5. Select OK to save changes and close the editor.

Task 9-17. Adding an Office Attachment Placeholder Definition

1. Use the Template Explorer to select a template into which you add placeholder definitions.

2. Select the `Placeholder Definitions` property in the Properties window, and open the Placeholder Definition Collection Editor.

3. Add an `OfficeAttachmentPlaceholderDefinition`. A generic placeholder definition is displayed.

4. Use the Placeholder Definition Collection Editor to set the properties of the placeholder definition:

   - **Description**: Enter a description.

   - **MustUseResourceGallery**: True|False.

   - **Name**: Enter a name.

   - **UseGeneratedIcon**: True|False.

5. Select OK to save changes and close the editor.

Task 9-18. Adding an HTML Placeholder Control

1. Use the Solution Explorer to navigate to and open a template file for editing. Select Design view.

2. Open the Toolbox and select the Content Management Server tab.

3. Place an `HTMLPlaceholderControl` on the template file.

4. Select the placeholder control, and set the properties:

   - **AllowHtmlSourceEditing**: True|False.
   - **EnableAuthoring**: True|False.
   - **EnableViewState**: True|False.
   - **ToolTip**: Enter a functional/operational description.
   - **Visible**: True|False.
   - **PlaceholderToBind**: Select Placeholder Definition.
   - **EditControlHeight**: Enter height.
   - **EditControlWidth**: Enter width.
   - **(ID)**: Enter a name.

5. Save changes to the template file.

Task 9-19. Adding an Attachment Placeholder Control

1. Use the Solution Explorer to navigate to and open a template file for editing. Select Design view.

2. Open the Toolbox and select the Content Management Server tab.

3. Place a `SingleAttachmentPlaceholderControl` onto the template file. This control appears as an image icon.

4. With this placeholder control still selected, set the properties of the control in the Properties window:

   - **EnableAuthoring**: True|False.
   - **EnableViewState**: True|False.
   - **ToolTip**: Enter a functional/operational description.
   - **Visible**: True|False.
   - **PlaceholderToBind**: Select Placeholder Definition.
   - **(ID)**: Type a name.

5. Save changes to the template file.

Note   If the Toolbox is not visible, click View ➤ Toolbox.

Creating MCMS Publishing Tasks

Publishing tasks describe specific Word UI and actions required to publish content to the site. A publishing task contains four tags:

- <name> contains the name of the publishing task.
- <description> contains a short description of the publishing task.
- <template> identifies a template from which the posting inherits.
- <channel> identifies the channel in which to post the content.

Publishing tasks are executed from the MCMS Authoring Connector Wizard. To create a publishing task, you must add a new XML tag that describes the task to a specific XML configuration file.

Task 9-20. Creating an Authoring Connector Publication Task

1. Open the publishing tasks file (\Program Files\Microsoft Content Management Server\Server\IIS_CMS\OfficeWizard\PublishingTasks.XML) using a text editor.

2. Add a new <tasks> tag:

```
<task>
    <name> [enter a name] </name>
    <description> [enter a description] </description>
    <template> [Enter the path to a template to use
for the publishing task] </template>
    <channel> [Enter the path to a channel to use
for the publishing task]  </channel>
</task>
```

3. Save changes.

Using the Web Author

An author creates and publishes pages using the Web Author.

Creating Pages

Use the Web Authoring console to select a template.

Task 9-21. Selecting a Template

1. Launch Internet Explorer.

2. Enter the URL of a template: `http://domain name/path`, where `domain name` is the address of the CMS site.

3. Select Switch to Edit Site.

4. Select Create New Page from the Authoring Console.

5. Use the Select Template Gallery dialog box to locate a template for the new page.

6. The template loads into the Web Author; enter content into the placeholders.

Placeholders streamline formatting, enforce consistency, and support authors. In many cases, content contributors are not authors in the classical sense. They may be sales associates, support personnel, or subject matter experts—people who have neither the skills nor the inclination to compose Web pages in the traditional manner. By merely entering highly structured data into placeholders, they can create, update, and publish content directly without the intervention of IT staff. Other nontechnical members of the content creation team can review and approve postings before they go live on the site.

Task 9-22. Adding an Image

1. Highlight an image placeholder.

2. Select Add or Edit Image to open the Select Source dialog box.

3. Select Insert Shared Image; the Select Resource Gallery dialog box is displayed.

4. Use the Select Resource Gallery dialog box to locate a Resource Gallery. The Select Image window opens.

5. Select the image from the gallery. (Select the icon under the Select column, not the image or name.)

6. Open the Insert Image dialog box and specify optional properties.

7. Choose the image, and select Insert.

To verify the appearance of your content, preview your page before saving and submitting.

Task 9-23. Previewing a Page

1. Select Preview in the Authoring Console.

2. The edited template is displayed in a child window.

3. When you have verified changes, close the window.

Task 9-24. Saving a Page

1. When you have finished using the Authoring Console to edit your page, select Save New Page. The Save New Page dialog box is displayed.

2. Name the posting and select OK.

3. Select Production Manager.

4. Verify Saved status for the new posting.

5. Close the Production Manager.

Publishing Pages

After a page has been created, it must be submitted for approval and posting to the live site.

Task 9-25. Submitting a Page

1. After the page has been edited in the Authoring Console, select Submit.

2. Select Production Manager.

3. Verify the new page status is Waiting For Editor Approval.

4. Close the Production Manager.

After you submit a page, you can set the publishing schedule to post the page to the live site. Editors and moderators generally set publishing schedules.

Task 9-26. Setting a Publishing Schedule

1. After you have used the Authoring Console to submit a page, select Page Properties. The Page Properties window opens.

2. On the Standard tab, select a Start Publishing option from the Publishing Options section (options include Immediately).

3. Select a Stop Publishing option (Never).

4. Save Changes, and then close the Page Properties window.

Note Subscribers cannot view published pages before the Start Publishing time or after the Stop Publishing time.

Task 9-27. Viewing a Publishing Schedule

1. Use the Web Author to locate a page.

2. View Page Properties.

3. Set the Start Publishing and Stop Publishing times.

4. (Optionally) Edit the Name and Display Name for the page.

5. Enable page options:

   - **Important Page**: Marks page as important.

   - **Hide When Published**: Hides the page on the live site.

   - **Web Robots Can Crawl Links**: Enables content search by Web search engines.

   - **Web Robots Can Index This Page**: Enables Web search engines to index content on the page.

6. Save or cancel changes.

Task 9-28. Approving a Page

1. Select Approval Assistant.

2. Go To approved pages, and verify changes.

3. Verify the publishing schedule.

4. Select the check boxes beside the pages to approve, and then select Approve.

5. Close the Approval Assistant dialog box.

6. Refresh the browser.

7. Verify that the page status is Published.

8. Select Production Manager.

9. Verify that the approved page is not among the pages in production.

10. Close the Production Manager.

11. Select Approval Assistant.

12. Verify that the approved page is not Waiting For Approval.

13. Close the Approval Assistant dialog box.

14. Select Switch to Live Site, and then navigate to the new page to verify it is on the live site.

Task 9-29. Using the Revision History to Compare Versions

1. In the Authoring Console, select Revision History.

2. View and compare previous versions of the page.

3. To view a specific version, select the View Revision icon adjacent to the desired version.

4. View Properties for a desired version.

5. Select Revision History.

6. Select the check boxes beside the versions to compare (Approved Revisions), and then select Compare.

   A child Revision History displays two selected versions.

Updating Pages

An author edits pages using the Web Author.

Task 9-30. Editing a Page

1. Launch Internet Explorer.

2. Navigate to the target site and page.

3. Select Edit in the Authoring Console.

4. The template is displayed with any content that has been previously entered.

5. Use the Authoring Console functions to edit the content, click Save, and then click Exit.

After the Web Author saves the page, it returns to Edit Site mode.

The page status Page Has Live Version is displayed.

6. Select Submit.

7. Select Production Manager to view pages currently in production.

8. Verify that the page's status is Waiting For Editor Approval.

9. Close the Production Manager.

10. Select Approval Assistant.

11. Check the box beside each page to approve and select Approve.

12. Close the Approval Assistant.

13. Refresh the browser, and verify the status is Published.

14. Select Switch to Live Site, and verify that the page has been published on the live site.

Task 9-31. Moving a Page

1. Launch Internet Explorer.

2. Navigate to the target site and page.

3. From the Authoring Console, select Switch to Edit Site.

4. Select Move.

5. Use the Move Page dialog box to select a destination channel.

6. Select OK.

You use connected pages to share content among pages.

Task 9-32. Creating a Connected Page

1. Launch Internet Explorer.

2. Navigate to the target site and page.

3. Select Create Connected Page.

4. Use the Create Connected Page dialog box to select a destination channel.

5. Expand the channel hierarchy and select the anchor page.

6. Use the Select Template dialog box to select a template (use the hand icon).

7. Select Preview to view the connected page.

8. Select Preview Connected Pages to view a list of pages connected to the anchor page.

9. Select Save New Page.

10. Use the Create Connected Page dialog box to name the new connected page.

11. Select OK to save changes (the Page Status changes to Saved).

12. Select Submit (the Page Status changes to Waiting for Editor Approval).

13. Select Approve (the Page Status changes to Published).

Task 9-33. Deleting a Page

1. Launch Internet Explorer.

2. Navigate to the target site and page.

3. Select Delete in the Authoring Console.

4. Select OK to verify the deletion.

The MCMS Authoring Connector

The MCMS Word Authoring Connector is a wizard-based application run from within Word. It allows you to submit, edit, or approve pages from within Word.

Task 9-34. Creating and Submitting a Posting

1. Launch Word.

2. Open or create a document.

3. Save the file.

4. Select File ➤ Send to MCMS ➤ Create New Page. The Authoring Connector Wizard opens.

5. Log on with authoring credentials, and select Continue.

6. The wizard displays the Publishing Task page.

7. Select a publishing task.

8. Create a page name. Check Make the Title the Same as Page Name (you may make the title different from the file name), and select Next to advance the wizard.

9. Enter Start and End information on the Publishing Dates and Times page.

10. Select Advanced Page Properties, and then click Next to advance the wizard.

11. Use the Advanced Page Properties page to set the following properties:

   • **Mark Page As Special Page**: Sets a graphic to mark the page as Important.

   • **Allow Web Robots to Crawl Links**: Enables Web search engines to search the content on a page.

   • **Hide Page from Subscriber When Published**: Hides the page from visitors to the live site.

   • **Allow Web Robots to Index This Page**: Enables Web search engines to index a page.

12. Click Next to advance the wizard.

13. Select Preview Page. The page loads in a new browser window within the Web Author console.

14. Close the Web Author when you are ready to publish the page.

15. Select Next on the Page Submission page to submit the page and advance the wizard. The page is now submitted for publication.

16. Select Finish to complete the wizard.

Task 9-35. Publishing a Posting

1. Launch Internet Explorer.

2. Navigate to the target site and page.

   • Select Edit Site mode, and navigate to the target posting.

   • Verify the Page Status is Waiting For Editor Approval.

   • Select Approve.

   Or

   • Use the Approval Assistant to check pages to approve and select Approve.

3. Verify the Page Status is Published.

4. Verify that the page is published by logging on as a Subscriber and viewing the page from the live site.

Task 9-36. Editing a Posting

1. Launch Word.

2. Open the Word document corresponding to the page that has been previously published.

3. Edit the document and save the changes.

4. Select File ➤ Send to MCMS ➤ Update Same Page. The Authoring Connector Wizard is displayed.

- Select Next on the Page Information page to maintain the same page options.

Or

- Use the Page Information page to enter new options.

- Select Next on the Publishing Times page to maintain the same publication options.

Or

- Use the Publishing Times page to enter new publishing times options.

5. Select Preview Page. The page loads in a new browser window within the Web Author console.

6. Close the Web Author when you are ready to publish the page.

7. Select Next on the Page Submission page to submit the page and advance the wizard. The page is now submitted for publication.

8. Select Finish to complete the wizard.

Summary

MCMS and Visual Studio provide an efficient development environment. Use Visual Studio to create an MCMS *application*. An MCMS solution provides a page-processing architecture that serves a unique bidirectional (presentation and authoring modes) Web-page model for managing content. The MCMS class library provides a *document object model* to facilitate automated publishing.

MCMS is template driven. MCMS template objects bind code and resources into dynamic pages. Placeholders structure data and make it easy for authors to contribute consistent content. Templates also facilitate content repurposing, which means the input template and output template may not always be the same.

Index

forums.apress.com

FOR PROFESSIONALS BY PROFESSIONALS™

JOIN THE APRESS FORUMS AND BE PART OF OUR COMMUNITY. You'll find discussions that cover topics of interest to IT professionals, programmers, and enthusiasts just like you. If you post a query to one of our forums, you can expect that some of the best minds in the business—especially Apress authors, who all write with *The Expert's Voice*™—will chime in to help you. Why not aim to become one of our most valuable participants (MVPs) and win cool stuff? Here's a sampling of what you'll find:

DATABASES
Data drives everything.

Share information, exchange ideas, and discuss any database programming or administration issues.

INTERNET TECHNOLOGIES AND NETWORKING
Try living without plumbing (and eventually IPv6).

Talk about networking topics including protocols, design, administration, wireless, wired, storage, backup, certifications, trends, and new technologies.

JAVA
We've come a long way from the old Oak tree.

Hang out and discuss Java in whatever flavor you choose: J2SE, J2EE, J2ME, Jakarta, and so on.

MAC OS X
All about the Zen of OS X.

OS X is both the present and the future for Mac apps. Make suggestions, offer up ideas, or boast about your new hardware.

OPEN SOURCE
Source code is good; understanding (open) source is better.

Discuss open source technologies and related topics such as PHP, MySQL, Linux, Perl, Apache, Python, and more.

PROGRAMMING/BUSINESS
Unfortunately, it is.

Talk about the Apress line of books that cover software methodology, best practices, and how programmers interact with the "suits."

WEB DEVELOPMENT/DESIGN
Ugly doesn't cut it anymore, and CGI is absurd.

Help is in sight for your site. Find design solutions for your projects and get ideas for building an interactive Web site.

SECURITY
Lots of bad guys out there—the good guys need help.

Discuss computer and network security issues here. Just don't let anyone else know the answers!

TECHNOLOGY IN ACTION
Cool things. Fun things.

It's after hours. It's time to play. Whether you're into LEGO® MINDSTORMS™ or turning an old PC into a DVR, this is where technology turns into fun.

WINDOWS
No defenestration here.

Ask questions about all aspects of Windows programming, get help on Microsoft technologies covered in Apress books, or provide feedback on any Apress Windows book.

HOW TO PARTICIPATE:

Go to the Apress Forums site at **http://forums.apress.com/**.
Click the New User link.